ISLAND
IN TIME

ALSO BY OLGA CARLISLE

Voices in the Snow
Poets on Street Corners
Solzhenitsyn and the Secret Circle

ISLAND IN TIME

A MEMOIR OF CHILDHOOD

Olga Carlisle

HOLT, RINEHART AND WINSTON
NEW YORK

Copyright © 1980 by Olga Carlisle

All rights reserved, including the right to reproduce this book or portions thereof in any form.

Published by Holt, Rinehart and Winston, 383 Madison Avenue, New York, New York 10017.

Published simultaneously in Canada by Holt, Rinehart and Winston of Canada, Limited.

Library of Congress Cataloging in Publication Data
Carlisle, Olga Andreyev.
Island in time.
1. World War, 1939–1945—France—Oléron, Île d'.
2. World War, 1939–1945—Personal narratives, French.
3. Carlisle, Olga Andreyev—Biography—Youth.
4. Oléron, Île d'—Biography. 5. Poets, Russian—20th century—Biography. 6. Children—France—Oléron, Île d'—Biography. I. Title.
D762.042C37   940.53'44'64 [B]   79-9434
ISBN 0-03-053326-0

First Edition

Designer: Amy Hill
Printed in the United States of America
1 2 3 4 5 6 7 8 9 10

FOR SASHA, AND FOR MY
FRIEND MARIE LUISE

I wish to express my gratitude to my editor, Marian Wood; and also to my husband, Henry Carlisle, whose help in giving form to my childhood story was invaluable.

The golden honey flowed so slowly
That the hostess had time to say: "Here, in
    Tauris,
In this melancholy land where we were
    brought by Fate,
We are never bored," and she looked over
    her shoulder.

Here, the rituals of Bacchus are celebrated,
And there are only guards and dogs. Like
    heavy barrels,
Calm days roll by. In the distance,
An echoing of voices, unclear, unanswered.

—Osip Mandelstam, *Tristia* (1922)

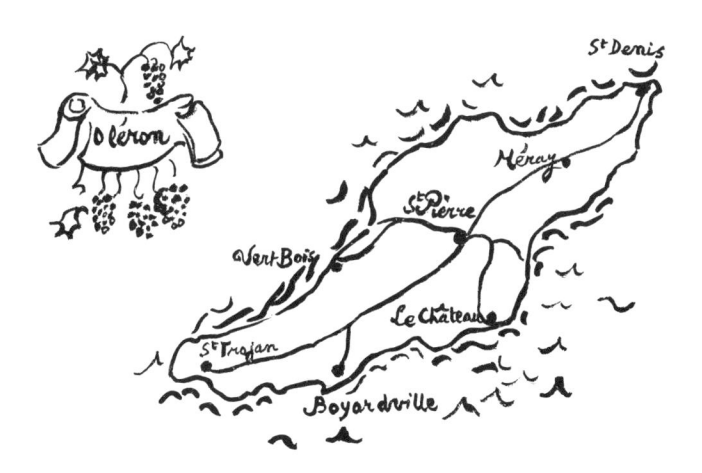

ISLAND IN TIME

Necklace of Bees

Except for a ribbon of litter—broken plastic bottles half-buried in the sand along the line of high tides—the beach at Vert-Bois, on the wild shore of the island of Oléron, has remained unchanged since the 1940s. Facing the open sea toward North America, it is still an unconquered expanse of glistening sand, so hard-packed by the tides that one's steps leave no marks on it. The wet sand, lightly veined with mysterious waterlines running out to sea, reflects the sky. The ocean is edged between two pale blue mirrors, a stately white mass of foaming water standing at the horizon. It fills the air with a low, even roar.

Looking out to sea, I wonder again, fleetingly, at the deceptive immobility of the tide. Waves are racing and catching up with each other. They are advancing imperceptibly. I know this and wonder: when will they engulf us? It is a long-forgotten sensation, the kind of pleasurable threat one relished in childhood.

ISLAND IN TIME

The beach at Vert-Bois on a late summer afternoon in 1939 is my first war memory: World War II had broken out that day. I was nine years old. We had come to the island of Oléron in the Bordeaux country that September for a month's vacation—seaside rentals are cheaper at the end of summer and, like most Russian émigrés, we were poor. I was not too surprised that the war had started. It was a catastrophe of course, unreal and yet inevitable. I was used to the idea of war; I had been brought up on war stories that had seemed appealing in the midst of our peaceful world. Throughout my childhood, episodes out of the Russian civil war had been interwoven with those from the Spanish civil war that was then taking place; both seemed legendary, a confrontation between good and evil full of medieval sieges and exemplary deaths, like the wars of King Arthur.

But the Russian civil war had been the very stuff of daily life. Stories about the civil war were stories of hunger—of having nothing at all to eat for months except frozen potatoes. Others were about street fighting, about police searches and daring escapes. These stories, involving my mother and her Socialist Revolutionary family, were improbable, fantastic, but through frequent telling they acquired a reassuring familiarity. And these tales had happy endings, since my mother and her family were there to recount them.

One year before, in 1938, when France and England had signed a peace agreement with Germany in Munich, I had been deeply struck by my parents' despair. At the age of eight, I came face-to-face with paradox: I understood that war was evil, and yet, I knew, too, that it should have been declared at once—for the sake of honor and also of survival.

We had no radio in the small apartment that we occupied in a distant suburb to the southeast of Paris, Le Plessis-

Robinson. At the end of each day, in search of news, my father and I walked up the town's wide main avenue. Usually we bought the evening paper, *Paris Soir,* and sometimes a Russian émigré paper as well. My father's sadness communicated itself to me. Outside the small stationery store where newspapers and magazines were sold, stacks of *Paris Soir*'s were laid out on the sidewalk under a striped red-and-white canvas awning. Inside, the store smelled of printer's ink. It was always crowded. People spoke to each other in loud voices; they were congratulating each other. Pictures of Hitler and Chamberlain, smiling and shaking hands, filled the newspapers. The headlines proclaimed in huge letters: WAR NARROWLY AVERTED! A NEW ERA OF PEACE! MIRACLE AT MUNICH! From that summer I have a recollection of flags and of patriotic parades—and of my parents' feelings of impotence and outrage. More than ever, we were strangers in France.

Because we were foreigners, a feeling of isolation had always been a part of my childhood. We lived in our own Russian environment, with its own language, in a new housing development hidden in the woods. Fifteen kilometers out of Paris, it stood on a hill above the forest of Robinson, famous in the nineteenth century for its treetop cafés where *midinettes* and painters had picnicked on Sundays. Built under the Socialist government headed by Léon Blum in the mid-thirties, Le Plessis was the first "garden city" in France. It was a spacious, geometric dream-city with uniformly square apartment houses intercepted with gardens, evenly disposed along very wide, empty avenues that were lined with newly planted plane and ash trees.

Few people lived in Le Plessis then. Its modest rents were

still too high for the French workers for whom it had been intended. By the late thirties, only a colony of Russian émigrés—artists and intellectuals—had moved in, along with a scattering of refugees of other nationalities, mostly anti-Fascists. Russians, Germans, Italians, and Spaniards lived side by side with an occasional family of French minor functionaries who, for their part, were bewildered by this airy, hygienic city of the future. For Le Plessis lacked the basic amenities of French life: it had no café.

There were forests all around us, and beautiful overgrown eighteenth-century parks enclosed by crumbling stone walls. In the woods one could find solitary ponds with poetic names like *l'Etang de l'écoute s'il pleut*, "The pond that listens to the rain." Our life was tranquil. But on Sundays when my parents held open house our apartment suddenly filled with friends who overflowed into the nearby park whenever the weather was fine. In addition to Russian and French, sonorous Italian and German were spoken by our guests. This filled our rare French neighbors with alarm; we were foreigners and bohemians.

An event which took place in the summer of 1939 had heightened our estrangement from the French world in which we lived. The Soviet Union had signed a bewildering, treacherous nonaggression pact with Germany. It had been a terrible blow to my parents. Once again Russia was dishonored.

We had a circle of friends made up of Socialists of varied backgrounds and persuasions. Some were Mensheviks, the splinter group cut off from the Bolsheviks in 1903. They had remained Marxists and were particularly affected. I remember long hushed conversations among adults, a stifled outcry, someone breaking down and weeping. Everyone we knew believed that Hitler had to be stopped and that time had all but run out to do this. However, to a number of undiscerning French people we now appeared to be Russians on Hitler's side.

It was on the very day of our arrival on the island of Oléron that we learned that a general mobilization throughout France had been called. We heard the news from the owner of the small stone cottage that we had rented in Vert-Bois, on Côte Sauvage, the wild shore of Oléron. She was a gruff peasant woman dressed all in black. She looked at us suspiciously. The house had been let to us by mail; perhaps she was surprised by our arrival on the island despite the outbreak of the war.

The war was on, irrevocably. My mother's reaction was one of anguish and disbelief. Standing in the small garden surrounding the cottage, she had, for a brief moment, refused to believe the news. The landlady was looking at us with hostility. We were on Oléron without my father; we were alone.

We left for the beach, my mother still on the verge of tears. As we walked through the fragrant pines in the golden midafternoon, I had the sharp feeling that the toy buckets and shovels which my brother and I were carrying were from now on ridiculously out of place, at least as far as I was concerned. My brother Sasha, only two years old, was oblivious to the events, though he had sensed my mother's anxiety at once.

I remember our first sight of the ocean. I had never seen anything as immense as the space which opened before us when we came out of the sheltering woods onto the dunes. It was filled with a blinding silver light. A steady wind, tasting strongly of iodine, blew from the sea. The three of us walked on the hard sand toward the water, three tiny dots in a shiny immensity. A foaming white wall stood in the distance. My disappointment at not finding the civilized attractions I associated with the lovely word *plage* (we used the French word for "beach" in Russian, and it was evocative of small, softly lapping waves) was almost as great as my concern for my mother. Her face, always gentle and vulnerable, was frozen with pain. My brother, who had never seen the ocean before, started to cry. I knew I had to forget the holiday pleasures I had dreamt of for so long.

Stays at the shore had been rare throughout my early childhood. However, one vacation at the seaside had left me with a passion for the sea. Sables d'Olonne on the coast of Vendée, where we had stayed in 1935, was an old-fashioned children's resort. Remembering the beach there as a place of enchantment, I had thought of nothing else for weeks before we set forth for Vert-Bois, although I had been warned that Oléron would not be as worldly as Sables d'Olonne.

While unfolding political disasters absorbed my parents, I was dreaming about the beach at Sables d'Olonne. There, a lively Avenue de la Plage ran along the water; its wide sidewalks were made of molded cement squares which looked like huge squares of milk chocolate. Along the Avenue there were merry-go-rounds and donkey rides for the children. Special stores sold fishing nets on long poles. Others sold toys for the beach, including gigantic beach balls, bigger than a standing man. One small shop had miraculous pale pink shell concoctions. Different varieties of tinted shells were glued together to form inkstands, picture frames, and boxes. Across them, elegant black slanting letters spelled out: SOUVENIR DES SABLES D'OLONNE. On a side street there was even a movie theater, which played what we called "fat man and thin man pictures"—Laurel and Hardy films. I don't think I had ever been to the movies before Sables d'Olonne.

In Sables d'Olonne, Avenue de la Plage overlooked a long curving beach of fine sand, particularly suited to the building of sand castles—or sand *pâtés*, as they are called by the gastronomically minded French. The beach was full of well-behaved children in trim bathing suits of nautical blue or bright red. High above the water stretched a row of cabins, pink and green wooden boxes whose doors were perforated with small heart-shaped windows. They were rented out to families for the entire season. To have the use of such a cabin for a whole summer had been my secret, unattainable dream.

Equally enticing were high-peaked, striped canvas tents, pitched far away from the transparent shallow water where children splashed. French mothers and grandmothers were settled in front of them on folding stools, knitting. Even in those distant days when formal attire was the rule for the French bourgeoisie, they were a strange sight, sitting on the beach in dark town clothes and hats. From afar, however, the vivid stripes of the tents absorbed them. They all but disappeared, becoming an innocuous part of the seascape. They seldom moved from their seats and, unlike my own parents, they never participated in their children's games.

In the mornings at Sables d'Olonne, when there were but a few children on the beach, the sea had sparkled, a promise of a radiant, endless day. In the afternoons, the French children were at last allowed to go swimming—four hours after lunch, their digestion presumably completed. By then the promise of an endless summer day had been betrayed; indeed, the day was finishing, but so beautifully that one was reconciled to this. The sun was setting over the sea; improbable pinks and purples appeared in the sky, and velvety shadows stretched farther and farther across a sand now deeply furrowed with footprints. The beach was then at its most exhilarating. Friendships between children begun that day grew and blossomed with the ending of the afternoon.

Alas, the beach at Vert-Bois on Oléron held no promise of

friendships. It was deserted, bordered by a low immensity of bluish dunes covered with coarse beach grass. The few bathing cabins at the edge of the dunes looked abandoned. As the menaces of war had intensified, the few Vert-Bois vacationers— obeying a call for self-preservation that had been the reverse of ours—had gone back to the city before the end of summer. We walked back toward the woods almost at once. I dimly knew that the beach at Vert-Bois prefigured our fate; like the war, the Atlantic Ocean was to rule our lives.

I remember little of the days that followed, except for the pines around our house and the house itself, so unlike any place we had ever occupied before. In a rush of recollections, the catastrophic events of World War I were coming back to my mother. That war had broken up her life, throwing her out of an idyllic childhood on the Italian Riviera into the rawness of Russia, an unfamiliar country in the throes of civil war. She tried to explain this to me, and I understood, more or less. I sensed that she was lost without my father, who had remained in Le Plessis. He was employed in a big rubber factory near Paris. Nor was there any prospect of his joining us soon, since the factory, which worked for the French National Defense, allowed no leaves at that time.

My mother's anguish communicated itself to my brother Sasha, who did not sleep at night, disoriented by the new surroundings. For the first two years of his life, in the calm of Le Plessis, he had led an existence of clockwork regularity. Now, while he dozed off in the daytime, my mother and I went for short walks in the woods. We explored its barely visible paths bordered with all sorts of plants that were new to me. To my mother, however, many were familiar from her years on the

Mediterranean, and she had a painter's attentive eye in observing them. There were bright blue thistles, their heads like medieval spike balls; tiny immortelles, an intense chrome yellow as they bloomed, while their faded counterparts, all fluffy, were a pale straw color and looked like ghosts of flowers. According to my mother, they would stay that way indefinitely, hence their name. The ethereal blossoms with their blue green stems could be made into bouquets, which would retain their dry, faintly bitter smell and light shapes forever; such a possibility seemed miraculous to me. Lovely also were the miniature pinks, their color a bright magenta, which smelled as strongly as full-sized carnations. Whenever the sun was out, the air in the woods was a mixture of immortelles, pinks, and warm resin, with a distant suggestion of seaweed from the ocean, and this new smell helped take my mind off the lost joys of Sables d'Olonne.

Freely, my mother discussed with me her immediate concerns—she had treated me as an adult from my earliest childhood. We had come to Vert-Bois ahead of our relatives in order to take possession of our cottage and organize our stay at the seashore, but now she was at a loss. Should we perhaps go back to Paris? Or wait for news from the rest of the family? A telegram from my father suggested that we wait for the arrival in Vert-Bois, within a few days, of my grandmother and of my aunts, Natasha and Ariadne.

During our walks, my mother spoke about the Italian Riviera where she had lived as a child—in the summertime it had smelled just like the woods around us now. She described with what expectations her parents, Victor and Olga Chernov, had departed in 1917 from Italy for Petrograd, via London and the Baltic Sea. Before the Revolution, threatened with arrest in

Russia because of their political activities, they had made their home by the Mediterranean. For years their house had been a center for underground anti-tzarist activity.

The news of the outbreak of the February Revolution had taken this family of Russian Socialists back home after decades of political exile. The adults in the family were elated at what looked like the dawn of a new era, while my mother and her sister Natasha, who had not been in Russia since infancy, were sad at leaving their Italian friends, and their house by the sea, which they were never to recover. But my mother's adoptive father, Victor Chernov, was being called back to Russia by the newly formed provisional government. An ebullient man, then in his middle forties, Chernov, a leading expert in the field of Russian agrarian reforms, was immensely popular within the Russian peasantry.

After the October Revolution had swept aside the provisional government, the Chernovs had gotten out of Russia against all odds. They had belonged to the Socialist Revolutionary party, the SRs, the non-Marxist, agrarian Russian socialist movement. Because they were a majority in Russia before the October coup d'état, the SRs had naturally been the Bolsheviks' most immediate enemies. Their extermination was started as early as 1918 by Lenin, later to be achieved by Stalin. But fortunately, Victor Chernov had fled the country in 1919. Olga Chernov and their three daughters, Olga, Natasha, and Ariadne, arrested by the Bolsheviks, had left Russia only in 1921—and only through an incredible succession of accidents and coincidences. On at least two occasions, at moments of heightened danger, they had fled the big cities, Moscow and Petrograd, to take refuge in the countryside.

I believe that my mother spoke of these distant events because she would not discuss a terrifying future with a child. A person of superior intelligence, with a highly developed imagination, she could guess what lay ahead for the world. She knew about the Allies' weaknesses, Stalin's duplicity, the American aloofness from European conflicts. The details of what was to come were lacking, as was an understanding of the scope of the events; in fact they were beyond anybody's imagination, and even my mother's, so very fertile, could not supply them. But the style of the epoch was set, it preordained the future; Hitler's hollow, absolute power over crazed mobs, the goose-stepping men of iron, the anti-Semitism.

My mother soothed us both by reciting poetry that she remembered by heart. My own diffuse memory of these days is forever associated with Mandelstam's *Tristia,* poems written at the height of World War I, which were attuned to our days on Oléron:

> Take for joy from my open palms
> A little sun and a little honey
> As we were ordered by the bees of Proserpine.
>
> No one can free an unmoored boat,
> Nor hear the shadow shod in fur,
> Nor conquer fear in the dense forest of life.
>
> We are left only with kisses,
> Prickling like tiny bees
> Which die when they leave the hive.
>
> They rustle in the transparent underbrush,
> Their homeland is Taygeta's impenetrable wood.
> Their food is clover, mint and Time.

ISLAND IN TIME

> Take for joy my wild present
> This plain dry necklace
> Of bees which died turning honey to sun.

We spent three or four days alone in the small house in the woods before my grandmother and two aunts with their children joined us, bringing with them news from Le Plessis and the world. The house was intriguing to an apartment dweller—a whitewashed building, roofed with pink Roman tiles. It was low, its doors opening onto a sandy garden planted with daisies and small climbing roses. Though protected from the sea winds by the pines, the house was damp. It lacked the comforts of our apartment, which until then I had assumed to be universal. There was no running water, no heat, no toilet. At some distance from the house stood two contraptions ubiquitous on Oléron. They were a massive stone well with a tin bucket on a chain running along a pulley, and farther away, a small wooden privy with a curious smell, a mixture of urine and warm pine needles.

At last one morning a big black taxi brought my grandmother, Olga Elyseevna Chernov, my aunts, Natasha and Ariadne, and their boys to Vert-Bois. Suddenly the cottage was filled with noise, and even laughter. There were now three very small boys racing in and out of the house in what seemed perpetual motion. They were Sasha, who was emerging from his state of despondency; Aliosha, his contemporary and best friend, my Aunt Ariadne's child, a wide-faced, Russian-looking boy full of vivacity and kindness; and angelic-looking, curly-headed Yegor, known as Kiska—"pussycat" in Russian. He was Natasha's younger son, the youngest of the three small cousins. Kiska was not yet two but he held his own bravely despite the

12

fact that Sasha and Aliosha often asserted their seniority ruthlessly.

The fourth boy in the family was Natasha's older son. André, two months my junior, was my constant companion. We had been brought up like brother and sister. Our mothers, Olga and Natasha, were twins, and they had acted as wet nurses for each other. André's presence broke the spell of foreboding in which I had become immersed. Playing with him, I was a child again. We were allowed to walk to the beach alone, he and I, and with our shovels tried to dig into the hard-packed sand. For a few days, something like a vacation at the seashore was conjured up for us.

After several evenings of emotional discussions among the adults, which we overheard from our beds, André and I realized that we would not return to Le Plessis that autumn. Everyone in

France recalled the Germans' ruthlessness toward civilian populations in the previous war. Bombardments of big cities were anticipated. My grandmother and her daughters—the Chernushkis (from Chernov), as they were collectively nicknamed—decided to settle somewhere in the country all together. Perhaps even on Oléron.

I was crushed. The thought of a long separation from my father was insufferable. I had cherished my life as my parents' only child until my brother was born in 1937, an event I had greeted with satisfaction, despite the fact that it had broken up the romance of Papa, Mama, and *dotchka* ("daughter"). Babies were a rarity in the thirties in France, and I enjoyed showing off my brother to my friends in Le Plessis. Sasha had been particularly endearing as an infant, lying under a white satin coverlet in a high baby carriage, which I was allowed to push when we went on walks in the park. This had filled the little girls of our neighborhood with respect and envy. That summer, however, my brother was growing into a little boy with a will of his own. In Vert-Bois that September, my childhood world was disappearing.

I could discuss this with no one, not even with my mother. I did not want to say anything that might upset her. Comforted by the presence of the other Chernushkis, she was beginning to recover her spirits. For the first time in my life, at nine, I *had* to act as an adult. Until then I had always had the choice whether to act as an adult or not, although usually I had favored the first role, so much more filled with interesting possibilities.

The Miracle Maker

A plan had to be worked out to get us into a more civilized environment. My grandmother, Olga Elyseevna Chernov, found herself once again at the head of the family in the absence of my father and my two uncles. My uncle Daniel, Natasha's husband, was being inducted into the army somewhere in the northeast of France. My other uncle, my favorite, Volodia Sossinsky, the husband of Ariadne, wanted to fight the Germans immediately. Because of his age—like my father, he was too old to be mobilized—the only avenue open to him was to volunteer for the French foreign legion, which suited his romantic inclinations. However, back in Paris, he was being delayed by endless bureaucratic obstacles. The *drôle de guerre* (the "phony war") was starting.

Having ruled out the thought of returning to Le Plessis, the Chernushkis were now feverishly trying to think of a thread which would help them find, in a village with a school and a doctor, a house large enough for all of us. Without some introduction, such a quest was inadvisable: at that moment, the anti-Russian sentiment of the average Frenchman was stronger than his anti-German sentiment. And, for all its wild, stylish beauty, Oléron appeared to be a closed community of grape growers and fishermen. Certainly we would not stay on in Vert-Bois.

My grandmother was a miracle maker. She was said to have the ability to solve seemingly insoluble problems through spectacular chance encounters and sudden inspirations. In addition to being a source of spellbinding tales for years afterward, this gift had been crucial in shaping the Chernovs' fate during the civil war.

Now, as we were sitting down to lunch in the tiny kitchen of the cottage, she suddenly remembered an acquaintance of hers, a Madame Desmons, encountered in the twenties during a vacation in the French Alps. Worldly, amusing in a dry, Parisian sort of way, Madame Desmons lived in Paris. She and my grandmother had tea together every year or so. My grandmother recalled that one of the subjects of her friend's tales was a brother-in-law, a country lawyer (a *notaire*). According to Madame Desmons, her sister's husband was a kindly but limited bourgeois, an embodiment of all the stock French provincial ridicules. My grandmother remembered that this brother-in-law, whose name she had never known, was established on the island of Oléron.

That very afternoon, my grandmother set forth on foot for Saint-Pierre, Oléron's main town, eight kilometers inland, at the very center of the island. In this tiny county seat, with its ancient whitewashed houses and narrow streets, she found the post office. There she asked for the name and address of the *notaire* of Oléron. She was told that there were two on the island, Maître Lutin and Maître Moquay. Their *études* ("offices") were at opposite ends of the island. Maître Moquay's was far to the south, in Saint-Trojan, and Maître Lutin's in Méray, in the northern half of the island. Not knowing which of these two lawyers might be Madame Desmons's brother-in-law, my grandmother decided to walk first to Méray, five kilometers away.

She found Maître Lutin's *étude* as it was closing. An aged clerk, sitting in a dark office lined with dusty legal volumes and mountainous piles of yellowing documents, said that, indeed, Maître Lutin's sister-in-law was Madame Desmons from Paris. In fact, had it not been for the "tragic events," Madame Desmons would be in Méray at this time of year, which she usually spent with her sister. My grandmother walked from the *étude* across an overgrown garden to the *notaire*'s large, sternly classical stone house. She found Maître Lutin and his wife at home.

My grandmother came from the Russian gentry. An ancestor of hers, Kolbassin, was a lieutenant of the seventeenth-century Ukrainian leader Mazepa. But despite her background, she was completely at ease among simple people, not only Russian, but also Italian and French. This was not an affectation on her part, although in her generation a "return to the people" had often been a pose. My grandmother genuinely found "ordinary people" absorbing. She had spent her childhood on her family's small country estate in the south of Russia and in Odessa, which had been, by the standards of those years, an open, cosmopolitan city—it had had notably a Jewish minority which was full of life.

In her youth my grandmother was to settle in the south of

France for a number of years. Her mother's family, the Suhomlins, had been exiled there from tzarist Russia. They were members of "The Will of the People," a populist revolutionary movement. Although he was personally uninvolved, my grandmother's oldest brother had been condemned to death after the killing of the tzar in 1881; spared at the last minute, he had spent fifteen years in Siberia.

Later, as the young wife of Victor Chernov, my grandmother had again lived in Italy and France. Her children were brought up in Europe and they too felt at home there, although the events of their adolescence in Russia—the unbelievable years filled with arrests, escapes, long periods spent in the underground—had made them more retiring than their mother.

Olga Chernov had lived through prison, famine, stretches of harrowing illegal existence during the Revolution, and the hard, arid years in emigration without losing her special, childlike strength. Her daughters, who loved her unconditionally, had helped sustain her. The passage from relative material security and public limelight into the bleak anonymity of exile was difficult for all the Chernovs. My mother and aunts developed a timid but very real practical sense, which balanced their mother's lightheartedness. This was particularly true of the older ones, the twins, who had had to go to work in the world of Paris couture at seventeen in order to support their mother and younger sister.

In spite of a painful divorce that took place at the height of the civil war in 1920, my grandmother's love of life never left her. During our Oléron years, at fifty or more, she was youth itself, with an absolute belief in her own indestructibility—and the infallibility of her intuition.

She was of middle height, a bit plump, with the beautiful

skin of a blond; in youth, her hair had been a dark blond and now she dyed it that color. She was very soignée, even during the years on Oléron when cosmetics were to disappear. Her clothes, usually made for her by her daughters, were discreet and becoming. Her manners were natural, yet she was distinctly the *grande dame* of our family. Toward relatives and friends she was attentive, tender, giving—though she never fully understood her older daughters' sacrifices on her behalf.

Despite her youthful years in Provence, my grandmother had remained in touch with her childhood in Russia. She knew about the secret wellspring of Russian culture, about what had been good there—and was then, and still is today. To my mind, she was the last person out of Russia with her inner freedom intact. She was in harmony with the essence of her country, although she came from a milieu whose mottoes had been self-doubt and an overriding desire for change. Unlike most émigrés, she felt no psychological gap between herself and Russia. (My own life of course, like my parents', was to be shaped by an awareness of such a gap, separating, unbridgeable.) Nor did she suffer from homesickness. Russia was always with her, even as she participated avidly in the life around her. Having never remarried, she surrounded herself with friends. Intense friendships with men and women alike were her element. All her effervescent charm and generosity came forth whenever an exalting friendship was involved.

In the middle twenties, my grandmother had lavished her time and whatever small amounts of money she possessed in trying to launch the émigré poetess Marina Tsvetayeva in Paris: Tsvetayeva had just arrived there from Prague. A great poet, a powerful but neurotic personality, the poetess treated my grandmother rather shabbily. My grandmother was deeply wounded, but she was resilient; for her, the world was filled with endless, uncharted wonders. After some months of despair, she forgave Tsvetayeva and turned to other friends. In the twenties, when they lived in Clamart near Paris, the Chernushkis held open house on Sundays. The writers Remizov and Zamyatin came, the poets Poplavsky, Ginger, and Bozhnev, and the painters Larionov, Goncharova, Ekster, and Falk. The marvelously witty, kindly Babel visited whenever he was in Paris.

In the thirties, my grandmother wrote for anti-Fascist newspapers. She had kept the idealism, the daring—and the lack of political ruthlessness—which had characterized the SRs. She was a member of the French Socialist party, the SFIO. Only a few days before joining us in Oléron, she had returned from an assignment in Italy, having gone there on an illegal trip to report on the politics of Mussolini's government.

All her life, Olga Chernov had wanted to be a writer. She had published several books—one about Rasputin, another about her experiences during the civil war. But she was not really capable of the prolonged effort literature demands. To her, all of life was a fabulous tale. Its episodes, one more intriguing than the other, were woven by her imagination into a sparkling fabric. Thus a routine event would take on a wonderful meaning, and she was able to convey her wonderment to others.

Unlike most raconteurs, my grandmother never repeated herself. As life went on, what she was recounting evolved, grew, took on new colors. Nor did she ever exaggerate—she was scrupulously truthful. It was only that she could record details which went unnoticed by others. And she knew how to listen better than anyone I have ever met.

Brought up in the loving but disciplined traditions of the

old equalitarian Russian intelligentsia, my grandmother appeared humble at times. She had no outward self-assurance at all—none of the messianic fervor that possessed so many of her generation. She liked to clean house and cook, which she did magnificently and very painstakingly. She loved to give presents, to entertain guests, to read to children. She was the flower of a civilization which, because of its openness, proclaimed more convincingly than any other in our time that life can be beautiful, that it is worth living to make it so.

My grandmother returned to Vert-Bois after nightfall. While the younger Chernushkis made evening tea, the ceremonial meal concluding a Russian family's day shortly before bedtime—that evening we still had real tea, and with it *petits-beurres*, and bread with jam—she told us about the long, windy road between Saint-Pierre and Méray bordered on both sides with endless rows of low vineyards stretching out to the horizon. To her, it had looked like Provence. The grapes were ripening; dark blue and golden bunches were hiding behind vine leaves, colored a bright turquoise by a copper spray.

Knowing of the ancient Mediterranean right for a passerby to taste discreetly of fruit from an unfenced orchard, my grandmother had tried of both white and black grapes. Fortunately, she was not seen. We were soon to find out that the customs of the Bordeaux country are different from those of Provence: grapes are sacred, untouchable in the Bordelais. In the Middle Ages, whoever stole even a single bunch of grapes had an ear cut off.

To the wanderer from Vert-Bois, Méray, with its towering elms, had seemed to hang forever on the horizon. When she reached it at last, it turned out to be only a very small village.

The houses' green shutters were still half-closed against the afternoon sun, but the dogs that had slumbered the afternoon away on the warm sidewalks were waking up. The cows were being brought home from the fields. A woman leading a single cow on a rope walked slowly by, her head lowered, knitting a woolen sock on fine steel needles as she went—a figure out of medieval France, with her long black cloak and her white hoodlike bonnet. In a voice heavy with the nasal, singing accent of Oléron, she had explained to my grandmother how to find Maître Lutin's office on a narrow side street.

The *étude* was marked by two highly polished brass disks decorated with figures in flowing robes holding up the scales of justice. My grandmother had found the office of the *notaire* claustrophobic, but his two-storied house across the garden, made of smooth white limestone, had French windows and an air of elegance. Inside, it smelled of cleanliness and wax. A glimpse through an open door revealed a kitchen with a row of glistening copper pots hung along the wall above a black cast-iron stove. But the parlor where my grandmother was taken at once was, according to her, a "pre-war nightmare," meaning of course World War I: she hated anything which reminded her of the constrictions of the Victorian era, such as long skirts and heavy furniture. Hung with portieres, the salon was crowded with monumental sofas and side tables covered with tasseled cloths. The yellow cherry furniture was polished to such a degree that the visitor had the feeling that someone in the household, perhaps the mistress of the house herself, spent her life shining everything about her.

Though surprised by her arrival, the *notaire* and his wife received my grandmother affably. Over the years, they had heard from Madame Desmons about her acquaintance with a charming and "very original White Russian lady"—for despite my family's struggle against the tzars for three generations, this was the category to which our family belonged during our years in France: white had been the color of the Russian imperial standard. And to the *notaire* and his wife, anyone arriving on foot from Vert-Bois at such an hour had to be "original"—this was a French euphemism for "eccentric." Fortunately, my grandmother had worn her most presentable outfit on her expedition, a light oatmeal-colored tweed suit. She had just bought it in Italy, and it breathed respectability and distinction.

A man in his early sixties, the *notaire* was exactly as Madame Desmons had portrayed him. Short, chubby, balding, with a bushy moustache across a ruddy face, he spoke in long sentences, using cumbersome legal expressions and referring to himself as *"le notaire,"* in the third person. And, as Madame Desmons had predicted, he was all cordiality. Upon hearing that my two uncles were *sous les drapeaux* ("conscripted")—and that my father was mobilized for National Defense, he immediately offered whatever assistance he could give to the families of worthy *défenseurs de la France en danger.*

Madame Lutin at first had been more reserved than the *notaire*. She could not have been more unlike her fashionable Parisian sister. As portly as her husband, she was in her middle forties. Her clothes had intrigued my grandmother. Madame Lutin was in dark gray, her costume all ruffles and tiny pleats, as if she were deliberately dressing for the part of a provincial lawyer's wife in a play. On her very plump legs she wore shiny black silk stockings; her frizzled hair stood up in a high, improbable coiffure. Underneath it she had a face that bespoke her kinship to Madame Desmons. Her features were finely chiseled and her eyes observing, intelligent, and not at all warm.

Then Madame Lutin's mother had come in. Madame Duval, the widow of a professor of history at the Sorbonne, was dressed like a Parisian of another age, without ruffles. She had reminded my grandmother of friends of her own mother's in their distant days in Provence, the faculty wives in the days of the Dreyfus affair, when the most polished gentlewoman would suddenly reveal herself in public as a fiery partisan of the unjustly persecuted Captain Dreyfus.

Despite its bourgeois atmosphere, there was something open about the Lutin household. And when the Lutins's son wandered in, he had seemed to come from another world altogether. Julien was a young man of eighteen or nineteen, as slender and aristocratic-looking as the *notaire* was plump and common. He had fine classic features, but there was far more softness in them than in his mother's.

The *notaire* made another little speech about how appreciative France was of my grandmother's sons-in-law, these valorous foreigners defending France in danger. He promised to help her find a house. Then he drove her back to Vert-Bois, to the edge of the forest where the asphalt road ended a short distance from our cottage. His white, top-heavy Peugeot could not venture onto the sandy forest road, but on the highway between Méray and Saint-Pierre it had swayed along at full speed, covering in a few minutes a distance it had taken my grandmother several hours to walk.

The *notaire* from Méray kept his promise. Within two days, he sent us word that he had found a house for rent on the northern tip of the island in the village of Saint-Denis. The following day he drove my grandmother and my aunt Natasha in the big Peugeot to inspect the house. It was a peasant's dwelling without modern conveniences, consisting of several oddly shaped rooms grouped around a primitive kitchen. The Chernushkis decided to take it anyway. Saint-Denis was a farming village opening onto a small harbor now invaded by sand dunes, a long stone jetty there still stretching far out to sea. In addition to a primary school and a doctor with a good reputation, it had marvelous beaches—three of them, each different from the other. Known as Saint-Denis-les-Bains on postcards sold there, the village had an air of gaiety despite its location on what was said to be the windiest end of the island.

On the following day, a clanking taxi of World War I vintage came up to our house in Vert-Bois, managing deftly on the sandy road. It was driven by a middle-aged man with a bright red face wearing a beret, Monsieur Glodon. Monsieur Glodon smelled of wine and of axle grease. He talked to himself endlessly, praising his taxi and the house he was renting us; he was to be our landlord.

The eight of us and all our possessions were loaded into the enormous auto and we drove off to Saint-Denis. On the way, the taxi broke down in a landscape of vineyards, curly-haired horsemen moving out to sea, an abandoned stone windmill, now wingless, relieving the evenness of the horizon. The sky above us looked enormous, bigger than any sky I had ever seen before. The ocean was too far to be visible from the road, but with the smell of seaweed it was everywhere, stronger and stronger as the island narrowed to the north. We had left the woods of Vert-Bois with their immortelles and thistles for a new country, windswept and bleak. I found it all desolate. Monsieur Glodon however was master of the situation. He tinkered with the motor for a long time, he cranked it, all the while talking to himself. We were on our way again in a cloud of smoke, with a great clattering.

I remember little of the inside of Monsieur Glodon's house in the heart of the village of Saint-Denis except for a vision of small children crying in unison in a dimly lit room with a concrete floor. The unattractiveness of the house was partly redeemed by its tiny yard. It was wedged between various outbuildings that came together at irregular angles, clearing a small triangular space in the center. The yard was cemented over and had zinnias growing out of tin cans arranged at the base of a beautiful old fig tree sprawling overhead like a huge tent.

The climate of Paris is too harsh for fig trees—I had never seen one before. The smooth gray trunk and the scratchy leaves with their cutout shapes filled me with joy. The smell of the leaves when they were crushed was like an expensive perfume. My clearest recollection of these days is sitting high up in this tree late one summer afternoon and becoming acquainted at leisure with the taste of fresh figs; until then I had only known dry figs in cellophane packages. Depending on their degree of ripeness, their flavor changed from a light flowery tartness when they were green to a rich red-and-golden mellowness and, when they started fermenting, to a winelike acidity.

In my recollections the taste of fresh figs is mingled with a sense of anxiety. I can still hear the voice of Edouard Daladier, France's premier at the beginning of the "phony war," when French and German armies stood still facing each other across the border.

Underneath me, somewhere, the Glodons' radio was going full blast. I felt doomed. I do not know now whether this was caused by an all-pervading apprehension or by Daladier's overblown oratory, which sounded false. I trace my first intimation that France might lose the war to that day.

I remember being ordered down from Monsieur Glodon's fig tree by my grandmother. There were admonitions to us children to behave ourselves—otherwise the French might think "that we Russians were savages."

But soon the Glodons' watchfulness across the small yard became oppressive to the Chernushkis. My grandmother started to look for another house. She agreed to take me along as she went off to discuss with Maître Lutin the rental of a big house bearing the sign *à louer*, which she had spotted near the harbor of Saint-Denis. It was known in the village as Maison Ardeber.

September was ending, but it still felt like summertime on the island that afternoon. For the first time, we walked the six kilometers between Méray and Saint-Denis along the asphalted *nationale* bordered by ancient elm trees—all the other roads in Saint-Denis were unpaved, brilliant white ribbons of limestone crisscrossing the countryside. Oléron was an island of silver in those years.

The straightness of the highway made it seem very long, but fortunately the *vendanges* ("grape harvest") was in full progress that week. Heavy horsedrawn chariots loaded with barrels were tied at the edge of the vineyards. Groups of men and women, using only pocketknives, each handling a row of vines, were cutting grapes with extraordinary rapidity.

We stopped to admire the intricate, staccato patterns of their work and the women's archaic-looking white bonnets, known as "kissnots," which went back to the English domination of the island in the days of Eleanor of Aquitaine. They were a protection, not only against kisses, but also against the sun and the clouds of tiny flies that swarmed around the workers and their horses. The air was filled with the vinegary smell of fermenting grapes. The sight of the opulent ripe bunches being harvested no longer tempted the passersby.

When we arrived at the Lutins, we were received by Madame Duval. The *notaire* and his wife had gone to a funeral. Madame Duval offered us a cup of tea and cookies in the big dining room. I was enchanted with the *notaire*'s house. The polished, sculptured Renaissance dining room furniture looked sumptuous. I enjoyed drinking tea like an adult with two ladies who included me in their conversation about the history of Oléron and Eleanor of Aquitaine. Fortunately, I had worn my best summer dress to the Lutins. Like everything I had, it had been sewn by my mother. Made of light blue linen, cut like a pinafore, it showed off my most prized possession, a small turquoise pin. This old Russian heirloom had been given to me by my godmother, Seraphima Pavlovna Remizov, the writer's wife. I liked fingering it. It made me think that our friends and our civilized existence in Le Plessis-Robinson would not be lost forever.

Despite my blue pinafore and my turquoise pin, I was not particularly pretty in those days. I was dark-haired and skinny. I was very proud of my resemblance to my father—I had his thick chestnut hair, his mat skin, and his agility; beyond this, I was not overly concerned with my looks. Above all, I was interested in appearing grown up.

After tea, Madame Duval led us to another part of the house, to the library in the back. It was unlike any library that I had seen before—differing from my father's with its slim paperbound volumes of poetry; or my godparents', the Remizovs, which was made of wooden packing crates overflowing with yellowing philosophical journals and thick, clothbound dictionaries. I was spellbound by the leatherbound volumes glistening all around the room. Madame Duval asked whether I might not want to borrow something to read. After consulting with my grandmother, she gave me Colette's *La Maison de Claudine* in a navy blue binding, promising to lend me another book on my next visit to Méray. I would have given anything to be allowed to settle in the library for the rest of the afternoon, but we were called back into the dining room. The Lutins had just returned from the funeral.

I was suddenly aware of how very informal we must have looked, my grandmother and I, in our summer dresses and espadrilles. The *notaire* and his wife were dressed in somber formal clothes, incarnations of old-fashioned French respectability. I had met the *notaire* in Saint-Denis before, but not Madame Lutin. She seemed even less appealing than my grandmother had described her, with her ironic eyes and some deep frustration under the polished exterior. Today, when I look at French sixteenth-century pencil portraits, I am reminded of Madame Lutin. The precisely drawn, aristocratic dowagers look across the ages with her insistent, doubting eyes.

After a while the Lutins' son, Julien, came in. At Madame Duval's suggestion, he offered to take me for a walk in the garden while the adults discussed the best way to convince a certain Mademoiselle Charles to rent us the house on rue du Port. Laughing, Madame Lutin was telling my grandmother about Mademoiselle Charles, "a church-going spinster with the brains of a sparrow."

I was pleased to go on a walk with Julien. He, like his grandmother, treated me as an adult—Madame Lutin had called me *"ma petite"* and even, for some reason, *"ma pauvre petite."* The garden where we walked was one of these exuberant French gardens laid out in the 1900s. Along its curving alleys it displayed one specimen each of various flowering shrubs whose names Julien told me in turn. The garden was dark and moist, but at its farthest end it had a clearing. There was a small orchard, bathed at that hour in warm yellow sunlight. In the middle of it stood a small tree loaded with *mirabelles,* the tiny, oversweet plums used for jams. They have the most intense color, that of a late summer sunset. Julien offered me a *mirabelle.*

He was a slender young man with narrow, smiling, enigmatic eyes. Everything about him was spontaneous and yet refined—even the way he walked, and the movement of his hands. He punctuated his conversation with humorous slang expressions I had never heard used before. He made slightly irreverent jokes about his father, whom he called *"le paternel."* Julien was the most attractive young man I had ever seen—more attractive even than Serge Efron, the soulful, gray-eyed husband of Marina Tsvetayeva, on whom I had had a crush a year before. I fell in love with Julien on the spot.

Every week in his white Peugeot, Maître Lutin came to Saint-Denis. The *notaire* held regular office hours in the Mairie ("town hall") on Wednesdays. There, the peasants, dressed in their Sunday clothes, discussed property matters with him. These were exceedingly complicated: for centuries intermarriage between islanders had been the rule. Hence, the endless sharing of fields: on Oléron no parcel of land was like another. Each could grow a certain species of grape best—differences in soil and in exposure made each absolutely unique.

The very first Wednesday after our visit to Méray, Maître Lutin called on Mademoiselle Charles. He explained that we were a respectable family of White Russians, but Mademoiselle Charles was reticent. We were foreigners of an alien, exotic faith. Moreover, her first cousin, the Docteur Ardeber who owned the house on rue du Port and now lived in Algeria, had specified that the house not be let to people with children.

The *notaire* assured Mademoiselle Charles that we were excellent Christians, almost Catholic in fact, had it not been for an unfortunate schism in the Middle Ages. My grandmother had had the good idea to explain to him beforehand that we were "Greek Catholics," rather than Protestants. On Oléron, once torn by religious wars, the antagonism of the Catholic ruling class against the Reformed church was still virulent.

Mademoiselle Charles remained evasive. Finally Maître Lutin reminded her that, should the Maison Ardeber be left vacant, it might be requisitioned without compensation to house refugees. At that, Mademoiselle Charles gave in.

The *notaire* was much pleased with his negotiations. Accepting a cup of tea in our kitchen at Monsieur Glodon's, he reported his negotiations in detail to the Chernushkis, whom he now called "The excellent Madame Chernov and the charming young ladies." We could move into the Maison Ardeber the following week. The monthly rental was high but still manageable. My uncles' army allocations were minuscule—we lived mostly on my father's earnings from the factory in Paris.

The deal was almost ruined the next day. That morning, my grandmother had taken my cousin André and me to the beach: the island was having a spell of Indian summer—some of my daydreams about Sables d'Olonne were coming true in Saint-Denis. We had started home at that fabulous midday hour at the seashore when the heat and the glare are at their peak and one feels all dried up by the sun, ready for lunch and a cool room in which to lie down. It was so hot that my grandmother allowed us to walk home in our bathing suits. We wore matching red, knitted shorts. Carrying fishing nets on our shoulders we were halfway up rue de Port when a gaunt lady in gray suddenly appeared. She wore a narrow skirt to her ankles and a black hat. She was walking toward us. Mademoiselle Charles herself.

My grandmother was about to greet her graciously when an icy stare emanated from underneath the hat. Mademoiselle Charles had stopped in the middle of the street. Her lips were pinched, her eyes disbelieving. A menacing silence was followed by a speech, delivered in a trembling voice, about the indecency of the costume of "these poor children." My grandmother had no time to say anything. Mademoiselle Charles sailed past us into a garden enclosed by a high iron grille.

But at four o'clock, when the Chernushkis called on Mademoiselle Charles to discuss the details of the rental, she said nothing at all about the noontime encounter. She only expressed the hope that *ces pauvres enfants* would do honor to their Russian upbringing, living as they would in a house exposed to public scrutiny. The Maison Ardeber on rue du Port was separated from the street only by a low stone wall.

Mademoiselle Charles had agreed to provide the Chernushkis with ancient quilts, eiderdowns, and heavy homespun linen sheets which must have been woven two hundred years before. With some hesitation, she pulled these treasures, smelling of camphor, out of enormous armoires. My mother and aunts reported that there was every likelihood that Mademoiselle Charles's house, located only a few steps away from the one we were renting, was haunted—it was full of dark corners and secret passageways. From that day on, André and I started dreaming about this house with its pale blue shutters, which we could only vaguely make out in the back of a junglelike garden filled with prickly exotic plants.

It was a cloudy, chilly Sunday afternoon in late November. I was hating Saint-Denis and the gray even surface of our life—as even and gray as the Oléron horizon on a sunless day. None of the promises of adventure and enlightenment contained in the books we read would come true. Oléron was our prison. That day, I was feeling especially sad. I missed my grandmother, who had returned to Paris to work there as a journalist. Without her, life was boring. And to make matters worse, I had quarreled with André, who had refused to lend me his roller skates. This was his right, there was nothing I could say; to bring in the grownups would have been undignified. I could only be offended by his silence.

That afternoon, leaving the sea, I walked along rue de la Muse, the main street of the peasants' part of town, running far inland. I had decided to find out how that seemingly interminable street, dating to another century, ended. I strolled for a long time, looking into unkempt, deserted farmyards. Evidently everyone in the village, even the usually alert Oléron chickens, was having a Sunday siesta. The shutters of the rare windows facing onto rue de la Muse were closed but for a narrow crack. From inside, they were held fast by heavy iron hooks. The peasants' houses were like miniature fortresses.

I had lost patience before I reached the end of the chalky street splattered here and there with cow manure. I started back along a side street, and found myself skirting a high wall. Tombs shaped like white candy boxes were visible above it. Smelling of nettles, a ditch ran alongside the wall, reflecting the lusterless sky. This was the village cemetery.

I had never been inside a cemetery before, though I knew what went on there from having read *Tom Sawyer*. I was tempted to go in, but the day was too mournful. Such an enterprise was best undertaken with André. I resolved to forgive my cousin as soon as I got home. And suddenly, as I reached the beginning of rue du Port, where the "Liberty Tree" grew—the centenary elm commemorating the storming of the Bastille—I saw Julien in the company of an unknown young man.

To see him, even at a distance, even fleetingly through a window of the Mairie where he sometimes helped his father on Wednesdays, was magical. Inside that drab, institutionalized room he looked like an exotic bird. Not that he wore anything special, but there was a lightness to his movements which was breathtaking. He was slightly nearsighted, and this added something both tentative and intense to everything he did. Sometimes Julien would not recognize people at a distance, but that day he made me out across the street and called to me.

Decorously, in the best style of French *comme il faut*, he introduced his companion, Maurice Desmons, to me. Julien's cousin Maurice, Madame Desmons's son, was a bespectacled boy of seventeen. The two cousins had just arrived on bicycle from Méray, where Maurice was spending a few days with the Lutins.

Within seconds Julien was inviting me to have some pastries at the Boulangerie-Patisserie behind the ancient elm. This was during the "phony war," and one could still buy everything in France. Inside the bakery, where on weekdays enormous freshly baked loaves were dispensed to a line of peasant women in black, every shelf was now filled with trays of pastries: creamy choux à la crême; pink and white, checkered Napoléons; glistening éclairs; Saint Honorés, all golden glaze over white foam. But it was not the pastries which made Julien's invitation so overwhelming. To be, however briefly, at the center of his attention was blissful. I relished each instant spent in Julien's company with the clear-headed rapture that one loses as an adult, when such sharply etched emotions become overshadowed by one's senses.

We stood inside the Boulangerie and ate two gâteaux each. Julien joked with Madame Bouchat, a kindly, tired-looking woman whose hair was lightly powdered with flour. I knew that Julien was unsure of himself in the face of the world, probably more so even than I, although I was dying of shyness. The slightly impertinent compliments which he was bestowing on Madame Bouchat were efforts at disguising his self-consciousness.

I felt it was imperative that I act as an adult on that day. In a manner no less dignified than Julien's, I asked the young men to stop by our house for a cup of tea. I could not bear to see Julien go back to Méray yet. They conferred briefly and accepted. Julien had Madame Bouchat fill a white cardboard box with pastries, which he chose with extreme concentration, as if he were arranging a bouquet of flowers. Then we went outside, where a strong wind smelling of seaweed was blowing. Julien made me climb on the luggage rack of his bicycle. I clung to him with one arm while holding the box of gâteaux under my other arm. Preceded by Maurice, who rang his bicycle bell gleefully, we rode toward our house. We passed a group of Oléronais out for a Sunday stroll, and my satisfaction at ignoring their astonished glances was almost as great as my pleasure in riding behind Julien.

It was important to me that all go smoothly with my friends on that afternoon. Fortunately, both my mother and Aunt Natasha were at home. A big copper vase filled with red oak leaves, which my mother and I had gathered the day before in the grove behind Mademoiselle Charles's house, stood in the center of the dining table at the Maison Ardeber. There was no sign of untidiness anywhere. It was not often so, and the usual disorder of our house had almost stopped me from inviting Julien and Maurice. I wanted everything concerning us Russians to be respectable, but now that the weather was growing cold, Sasha, Aliosha, and Kiska played indoors most of the day. The boys liked to overturn furniture in order to build imaginary houses and automobiles. Mercifully, they were now on a walk with Ariadne. André had gone off with them.

My mother came downstairs first to greet our guests. She lit the low-hanging lamp with its shade of green glass that hung over the table. Covering the table with the stiff damask tablecloth given to us by Mademoiselle Charles, she put out the gâteaux on a big platter. I was proud of my mother. In addition to being, in my opinion, one of the brightest people I knew, she always looked pretty. Regardless of what she was doing, she dressed becomingly and wore her dark blond hair neatly combed in pageboy fashion. She did even the most menial tasks around our new home, such as washing clothes or scrubbing floors, with a certain dainty efficiency. In this she was like my grandmother, and I, who regarded the female condition as generally unenviable, made an exception of them.

Around the house Natasha was less stylish than they. She wore comfortable, warm slippers and a knitted jacket, but I had to recognize that on festive occasions, she had more éclat than my mother, although they were twins and looked so much alike that they were often mistaken for each other. And, indeed, Natasha came downstairs looking beautiful in a big white shawl flowered with magenta roses. Once again we were having a party, as we used to have on Sundays in Le Plessis. The Chernushkis and Julien discussed the people whom we were getting to know around Saint-Denis. Julien gossiped about the Bourrades, the very proper family of a retired colonel who had settled in a large Victorian house on the outskirts of the village.

I listened intently. I was fascinated by the Bourrades. They had two teen-aged daughters, Roberte and Gigi, who went around the village on new, shiny, gunmetal bicycles with balloon tires. They were said to have tutors coming in every day from Saint-Pierre to give them lessons.

I was hoping to learn more about the Bourrades, but there was a commotion in the garden. Ariadne and André had returned from their walk with the small boys. Looking at André as he walked in, I knew that the roller skate incident was forgotten. André and I were friends again.

My Aunt Ariadne was then in her late twenties and looked like a slender, well-mannered adolescent. She had wide cheekbones and eyes ever so slightly slanted upward, which her son

Aliosha had inherited, along with her even disposition. Her long, light brown hair was tied back in an old-fashioned bun. Ariadne was elegant, composed, and endlessly patient with children. The little boys in our family, often boisterous when they were all together, obeyed her; yet of the three shy sisters, she was the shyest. She made one think of a smooth, sea-polished stone.

After their share of pastries was distributed to the smaller children, they were sent upstairs to play. The conversation turned to poetry, comparing Russian poetry with its richness of sound with French poetry, full of clarity and order. Julien declared himself a partisan of Gallic precision, but he listened avidly to what my mother and my aunts had to say about Russian verse. His bantering tone vanished, he was now full of fire—Julien was a poet.

I was even more taken by this new Julien than by the other, lighthearted one. My father was a poet, and Russian poetry was our blood, our point of view, our anchor in the seas of emigration. I was full of appreciation when, for Julien's benefit, the Chernushkis as a trio undertook a spirited defense of Russian poetry. Losing her restraint, even Ariadne joined in.

My mother and her two sisters were very close. They had married men who were intimate friends and had children close in age. They cared immensely about each other's opinions as against those of an alien outside world. Whenever a subject of conversation engaged them, they talked with great ardor, interrupting each other at an accelerated and somehow disconcerting rhythm—one best captured, I now recognize, in certain Chekhovian dialogues. Together they were charming. I felt a vague jealousy as well as satisfaction at seeing Julien fall under their spell, though he ardently defended the preeminence of French poetry.

I had never before heard French verse read aloud. I was overwhelmed when Julien, in answer to the Chernushkis, quoted a fragment by Valéry in a quiet, almost prosaic fashion. It was about the sea, which now dominated our lives:

> I am the blue. I come from the lower world
> to hear the serene erosion of the surf;
> once more I see the galleys bleed with dawn,
> and shark with muffled rowlocks into Troy.

Her eyes shining, Ariadne responded with a poem by Tsvetayeva, which the other Chernushkis translated into French for the benefit of Julien and Maurice:

> Eyes full of tears,
> of rage and love.
> Czechoslovakia in tears
> Spain losing blood.
>
> Black mountain
> darkening the world.
> —Creator, I return
> my ticket to Thy world!

Ariadne recited in a ringing manner. Into our idyllic afternoon, war and a premonition of tears swept in. Our friend Marina Tsvetayeva had gone to Russia a few months before. We would never see her again—she was to commit suicide there in the summer of 1941.

The mood of our tea party grew in intensity as more poems, French and Russian, were recited, but it ended on a light note. Startling everyone, the little boys came downstairs with a great clanging of toy weapons and drums. They were storming the dining room full of Germans. To the Chernushkis' distress, they often played war. Soon it appeared that Julien and Maurice were not above playing children's games also. Everyone, including Kiska, participated in a wild game of tag while the Chernushkis put tea things away in the kitchen. Breathless from the running, the young men suddenly realized that they were late: dinner at the *notaire*'s was served promptly at quarter to eight. We said good-bye in the garden, where one could faintly hear the pounding of the surf against the jetty. Julien promised to return soon and to bring us a supply of books.

Julien kept his word: one afternoon, in a big oilcloth shopping bag hooked to the handlebars of his bicycle, he brought us a leatherbound edition of *Little Dorrit* and Edgar Allan Poe's stories in a translation by Baudelaire. He said that he would come back soon for a visit, a promise he did not keep for a very long time. Perhaps Julien was not the clear-eyed Prince Charming he had appeared to be on that late summer day when he had taken me on a tour of the garden in Méray. He was by nature elusive. He was Madame Lutin's only solace in a confined, provincial world. Because he was extremely serious about his writing, Julien needed us as much as we needed him, our purveyor of books and our one friend with an insider's knowledge of the island. But soon he found himself playing intricate games in an effort to conciliate the world of Méray and that of Saint-Denis. Julien was forever torn between a desire to please and a desire to escape. He liked mystifications. He would disappear from our lives for weeks with some fantastic excuse, or without any explanation at all.

That first winter in Saint-Denis, while listening to *Little*

ISLAND IN TIME

Dorrit, which the Chernushkis particularly liked, or daydreaming about Julien, I sometimes tried to draw pictures with the pastels my father had sent from Le Plessis, but somehow they did not come off. I had lost the spontaneity that had made drawing a joy only a few months before. Now I turned to books.

I remember the cold—and the immense Ardeber beds of dark mahogany, with their high, curved headboards and their perpetually damp horsehair mattresses covered in faded chintzes. Yet they were the best place to read, despite one's icy nose.

In addition to some old comic books we had found in the Maison Ardeber—albums about Bécassine, the silly Bretonne maid, which were frowned upon by the adults for their lack of social conscience—I read all of Edgar Allan Poe's stories. André also liked Poe. "Ligea," "Morella," and "The Fall of the House of Usher" became part of us. On a winter night, all of Saint-Denis, the Maison Ardeber, and even our own bedrooms looked like settings out of Poe. We were thrilled to be the inhabitants of such a disquieting domain.

The House on Rue du Port

The house on rue du Port had an enigmatic quality, which grew instead of being dispelled as we went on living in it. Whitewashed and pink-roofed, it was bordered by a small garden fenced in by a wall, low enough for the small children to climb on easily. By day the house was cheerful, open to the outside world, yet its thick walls had capricious outlines. Little by little, we realized it was but one in a complex of buildings that had once formed the Charles estate. André and I became curious about the Charles family.

Before the phylloxera had destroyed Oléron's vineyards at the turn of the century, the Charleses had been wealthy landowners. Later, their half-farm, half-manor had been divided into three houses, known respectively in Saint-Denis as the Maison Charles, the Maison Masson, and the Maison Ardeber. Nowadays, going from one to another directly could only be done by climbing on the roof and crossing wide tiled expanses.

The rounded Roman tiles had a way of splitting with a soft, purring noise under our steps, while we studied the former Charles estate from above.

The manner in which various walls had been set up suggested that there had been hostility between the Charleses' descendants. The weapon of warring provincial families—not speaking to each other for decades while living side by side—was used by Mademoiselle Charles and her first cousin, Monsieur Masson, a thin, immensely tall bachelor who lived next door to us behind perpetually closed shutters. As the war went on, Mademoiselle Charles softened her attitude toward her relative. One day, meeting her cousin on the street, Mademoiselle Charles spoke to him within sight of the whole neighborhood.

From the reaction of everyone on rue du Port, we knew that an important event was taking place, as the cousins faced each other stiffly in the middle of the street. Our neighbors peered from behind their lace curtains. Suddenly, they were called outside by urgent domestic tasks, stepping out to shake a rug or to sweep the gutter that conveyed waste waters along the street. They were intent on observing the first exchanges to occur between a Charles and a Masson in more than thirty years.

The two cousins looked ridiculous to André and myself. We did not know that they were the last representatives of a France disappearing under the catastrophic blows of the twentieth century. They were stylish and pathetic, both dressed in black clothes turning green with time. As they conversed in the lazy Oléron midday, during that hour preceding lunch when the French relax in anticipation of the main event of the day, Monsieur Masson was waving his long thin arms and explaining to his cousin that prosperity was once more within reach for

Saint-Denis. All it would take was the building offshore of a second jetty perpendicular to the existing one. This would result in the washing away of the sand which now filled the village's dead harbor. Monsieur Masson had spent his life studying the tides around the northernmost tip of the island beyond Saint-Denis. The building of a second jetty had become an obsession with him, and he tried to impart it to whoever would listen.

The Maison Ardeber had an excellent observation post from which to study the life of our neighborhood. In the center of our densely planted garden—there were plum trees and laurels, and a flowering chestnut—an enormous yucca grew. Its leaves were as sharp as knives, darting upward in murderous rings of spikes. Once in a while, this centenary tree sent great asparaguslike shoots upward, which turned into creamy white blossoms. Like Monsieur Glodon's fig tree, the yucca provided a spot for secret observation. It had the advantage of being an armored stronghold; one had to know how to crawl safely around the threatening, shiny leaves.

The younger children were forbidden to climb on the yucca; in any case, they preferred the garden wall as a post from which to study the various activities of rue du Port. They were fascinated by the town crier who, once or twice a week, made public the governmental ordinances that were imposed on the civilian population as soon as the war began. With a huge drum settled on the handlebars of his bicycle, he traveled to the various sections of Saint-Denis, making a stop every two or three hundred meters. Beating out a roll, he read the new dispositions in a monotonous, barely intelligible voice, while the people of the neighborhood slowly assembled to hear him out, and then lingered on in the street, discussing them guardedly.

The town crier was said to have been the victim of a childhood accident. Or had he been wounded in World War I? No one knew for sure what had left him disfigured. He had a red, flat face without a nose. This awed the small boys, who decided that the town crier had fallen into a fire as a child. He had a speech impediment, and it was hard to understand why he was assigned to the particular office he held. In the village, he was taken for granted; everyone was used to his strange elocution. To me, he was frightening—a faceless prophet with a drum.

A laurel hedge screened the depths of our garden from the street. Behind it towered a metallic contraption, a water tank with a pump attached to it. By pumping energetically into the tank, one had water flowing out of a faucet into a hand-carved stone sink in the kitchen of the Maison Ardeber. To be sent out to pump up some water for kitchen use—fifty, seventy, or even one hundred strokes—was a chore, but not without its compensation. Prolonged, rhythmic pumping was conducive to deep thinking, especially at dusk. It helped one to sort out thoughts— and there was much to think about in those days.

I had the feeling that, with proper concentration, any riddle could be solved. All that was needed was time enough to think it through. I thought that the answers were already there, hidden somewhere in the depths of the laurel hedge. If only one could discover the right question, its answer would naturally emerge out of the fragrant darkness.

Near the pump stood a high wall that ran at a right angle to the street. It was made from cement blocks arranged into a ladder pattern, which made it possible to ascend it whenever one wanted to pursue one's thoughts undisturbed. This "thinking wall" cut the garden in two. On the other side was a second garden, which we progressively annexed in our slow, irrepressible occupation of the old Charles domain. Julien declared delightedly that we were invading Huns rather than proper White Russians—a joke which annoyed me.

I loved the Maison Ardeber, it was a house filled with promise of adventure. We were persuaded that, with their unaccountable protuberances, its walls held hidden treasure. Or else the treasure might be buried in the oak grove behind Mademoiselle Charles's garden. André and I made several preliminary excursions there trying to locate the spot where we might dig for it. We also spent a lot of time tapping the walls of our house for hollow spots. We were looking for a chest containing documents that would throw some light on what lay in store for us.

In advance, we savored the thrill of sharing our find with the adults.

At the time, it had seemed that only a bit of accidental procrastination prevented us from making that discovery—daily events distracting us in our search. We had assumed that the Maison Ardeber would be ours forever. Or was it a fear of being faced with some disturbing revelation which had kept us from pursuing our quest to the end? Instinctively, we acted like the Chernushkis, who had opted for passivity when they decided to stay on Oléron at the beginning of the war. In those years, people were frequently possessed by the opposite urge, a compulsive desire to move on, as if somehow one could escape war and one's fate.

Like many adults in Europe seized by madness, André and I spent a great deal of time telling fortunes, dripping hot candle wax into water and interpreting signs. This was a period when the predictions of Nostradamus were revived and swept through France; the Apocalypse was frequently quoted.

My mother maintained that Mandelstam had written about us in his *Tristia*, when he had celebrated the rituals of war as they are enacted by women and children, those who do not fight in battles:

> I have studied the science of separation
> between the tangled tresses of the night.
>
> This is how it will be: a transparent figure
> lies on a clean clay platter,
> like the small, flattened skin of a squirrel.
> Over the wax, attentive,
> a girl is watching.

> To fathom dark Erebus is not for us:
> wax is to women what bronze is to men.
> We meet our fate in battle
> but she will die, telling the fortunes.

I found this poem unsettling. It was the flattened-out figure on the plate that contained the answer to my questions, and I did not want to seek it there. I would have preferred to go into battle like a man.

One day in the early part of that winter, the beaches at the end of rue du Port suddenly looked like miniature arctic seascapes. We were astonished: the Atlantic Ocean began to freeze, the crests of the weighty, rapidly moving waves were turning to frost in mid-air. Sparkling ice floes were rushed to the shore by the surf, to be crushed there in a joyful, rhythmic commotion.

Even the imperturbable Oléron fishermen whom we met on the beach were bewildered. They could recall nothing of the sort happening over many decades, although, if one conversed with them one discovered that Oléron's past abounded in half-remembered, strange events. There had been an earthquake that had hit the island in the eighteenth century and, sometime before that, a sack of Le Château by Moorish pirates. More recently, a murderous wild boar had haunted the woods of Vert-Bois.

When oysters broken off the limestone rocks by the frost began to wash onto the hardened sand, the fishermen warned us that these were poisonous. We were accomplished gatherers of mushrooms and barnacles, André and I. We could not resist collecting the frozen oysters also. We brought them home and the adults tried them, reluctantly at first: they were delicious.

We ate them without any ill effect. When we later told Julien about this he was horrified. He attributed our survival solely to the fact that Russians had stomachs like ostriches.

All too soon, the polar fairyland, the result of some complex temperature pattern, was gone. The crystal seascape faded so suddenly that we began to think we had dreamt it. An endless succession of cold, sobering days followed. A steady north wind whipped the sea day and night for many weeks.

One evening after dinner, as André and I were about to go to bed, my father walked into the Maison Ardeber. He wore a bandage on his left hand. He had had an accident at the rubber factory where he worked: his ring finger had been crushed by an iron bar. This had put him out of work for several days. Instead of alarming my mother with letters about an accident, he had decided to visit us on the island. He was to stay with us for six days. To me, those days were like a lifetime.

I hated the feeling that I owed the delight of being with my father to a wound. Why could he not have come to stay with us before it had happened—come to stay with us for good? My father explained that he had no right to leave the factory at that time. He was mobilized there like a soldier, which he was to become in June.

When I heard about this, I was filled with terror. I had a notion that the chances for a soldier *not* to be killed in war were small, and this was already causing me to worry secretly a great deal about my two uncles who were stationed on the German front. All my life, I had seen monuments to the victims of the Great War in the center of every French town square. They had long lists of dead men chiseled into the stone. Below, sorrowful limestone soldiers looked like oversized toy soldiers in their flat helmets. They raised their eyes and their arms toward an unconvincing symbol of triumphant France, a bronze rooster perched on one leg and known as *Coq Gaulois*.

I tried not to think about the war: my father was with us. It seemed to me that to be with him was all I wanted in life.

He loved everything about Saint-Denis on this first encounter with our island, especially the sea. Life on Oléron fitted him to perfection physically and mentally, while the Chernushkis were relieved to have a masculine presence in the household, however briefly. I had not seen my mother smile as happily since we had left Le Plessis. Several times a day, she and my father strolled down to the jetty to look at the ocean. My father had been brought up on the Gulf of Finland; he loved the sea, like his father before him.

My father was the oldest son of Leonid Andreyev, a Russian playwright who had been famous just before the Revolution—he was the author of *He Who Gets Slapped* and *The*

Seven Who Were Hanged (an indictment of capital punishment). Andreyev—beautiful, talented, somber—had been one of the last romantics of Russian letters, a tradition that started with Lermontov and ended, quite recently, with the death of Boris Pasternak. Everything Andreyev did was elegant and somehow bigger than life. His love of the sea was passionate, and the wooden mansion he built on the edge of it was melancholy and magnificent. In it he mourned his "lost Lenore," my father's mother, Alexandra Viligorskaya, who had died when my father was only five years old.

Andreyev's involvements were all intense and exemplary: his friendship with Maxim Gorky, in which Gorky took the part of social consciousness and political engagement, while Andreyev spoke for the responsibilities and rights of the individual; his political stand against the tzarist pogroms; and, just before he died in 1919, his vehement denunciation of Lenin's terrorist methods.

My father's isolated childhood by the sea, in the company of his brooding father, made the remoteness of Oléron and its roughness somehow familiar to him. On the other hand, from his mother, a descendant of the national Ukrainian poet Taras Shevchenko, Vadim Andreyev had inherited a capacity for joyfulness and an even disposition, which contrasted sharply with his father's pessimism. This stability made it possible for him to conciliate throughout his life his writing with various full-time jobs with which he supported us, and to enjoy the pleasures and the turmoil of a house filled with children.

Although my father's hand was still hurting him and he had to wear his left arm in a sling, we did manage to go on several expeditions. These first, windblown explorations of the island made us feel like its sole masters.

A walk along the northwestern shore, known as Côte Sauvage ("the wild shore"), lasted a whole day. There, a spectacular beach curved to the south as far as one could see. It was made of the finest white sand, separated from the dunes by a snowy ribbon of round, white stones running to the horizon. One day we went all the way to Vert-Bois. The waves there in the winter were colossal, white foamy walls racing toward us in close formation. Once again, I felt a hatred for the sea and the war which imprisoned us.

In the evenings while my father was still with us, there were conversations about the war. The adults were horrified by the campaign launched against Finland by the Soviet Union that December. They called it infamous. They also discussed the ominous immobility of the French–German front—the French were calling this state of affairs *l'expectative militaire*. While volunteer groups made plans to beautify, with rose bushes, the Maginot Line—the French line of fortifications along the Rhine—military authorities were said to add bromide to the soldiers' rations in order to pacify them.

During his visit with us, my father reread our favorite author of that moment, Edgar Allan Poe. Ever since his own somewhat gothic childhood in the enormous wooden mansion in Finland, he had liked Poe. He told us all sorts of things about the American poet, about his opium smoking, and his love for his child bride, Lenore.

One day he joined us on a treasure hunt in Mademoiselle Charles's woods. We wanted to survey her oak grove before deciding where to dig for a chest full of gold and esoteric manuscripts. We all but decided on a certain spot, and only the lack of a shovel had prevented us from starting our digging that day.

On the way back from our expedition, we ran into our landlady. My father introduced himself to her, and she was clearly pleased by his courtly manner. She was untroubled by the fact that he spoke French with an accent and an occasional grammatical mistake. Unlike the Chernushkis, who knew several languages perfectly, my father had always maintained that, to keep his Russian alive for the purpose of writing poetry, it was better for him not to study other languages. But despite his fanciful French, there was nothing of the poor émigré about my father. He was an elegant man, athletic, with finely drawn, yet strong features. He looked dashing and respectable at the same time. He had what André described enthusiastically as "a proud walk."

Mademoiselle Charles was happy to meet a responsible-looking male member of our family. It seemed that she had been criticized in the village for having rented her cousin's property to "foreign ladies." The fear of spies was intense on the island. Two women of Spanish origin who had taken refuge in Méray had recently been accused of transmitting messages to the Germans in Morse code. Fortunately, when the gendarmes looked into the matter, it turned out that they had only been practicing ballet steps in the barn behind their small house. Foreigners were a strange lot: Mademoiselle Charles would have been astonished had she known that this distinguished-looking White Russian had just been investigating her woods for a treasure buried there by pirates.

At first, for us the war had been like a huge, smooth sea. We were becalmed in the middle of a treacherous element, which might engulf us at any moment: all the young Chernushkis could do was to try to create for our family a cheerful day-today existence. My father's presence had brought some comfort to them. And he had decided that, in order to hold our own in Saint-Denis, we had to have bicycles. André agreed: he knew that one's status on Oléron depended on owning a bicycle, known as a *clou* (a "nail"), no matter how rusty and squeaky. Before leaving, my father promised André that he would ship us our old bicycles as soon as he returned to Le Plessis—alas, there was no question of getting silver bikes with balloon tires like those of the Bourrade girls. My father said that he would also send along a tricycle for the small boys. It had been given to my grandmother for them by a new friend of hers, a young Italian woman whose son had outgrown it. My grandmother now often mentioned this friend in her letters. Her name was Clara Rittoni.

Clara and Paul

That spring, in a sudden crescendo of terrifying news about the Germans' advance into France, the "phony war" became the *guerre éclair* (the "lightning war"). It was hard for us on Oléron to understand what was happening. We did not know that, in fact, no one in France understood, and least of all the French high command. Every day the newspapers looked more ghostly. Their white, censored spaces grew as the French armies began retreating. The news via the radio was more candid than in the papers. Knowing that we did not have a receiver, Mademoiselle Charles invited us on occasion to listen to hers in her dark salon where it stood on a carved side table, an object endowed with special powers, a link with the world that the more affluent islanders had acquired only a few years before.

Panic was seizing France but Saint-Denis was calm. Not since the seventeenth century had Aquitaine been at war. No one on our island could believe that the Germans might reach

Oléron. Only the refugees would be a problem. In the sunshine, Saint-Denis looked like a sleepy summer resort. This was a look I loved. The souvenir shop above us on rue du Port, closed all winter, reopened, and it had toy sailboats in assorted sizes for sale, and revolving racks of color postcards with views of our beaches. I kept sending blue seascapes stamped SOUVENIR DE SAINT-DENIS-LES BAINS to my father and to my grandmother.

Huge defeats bearing the names of famous French victories—the Marne, Amiens, Verdun—punctuated that spring. Once, from my vantage point in the yucca, I saw our neighbor from across the street, Colonel Merle, walk along rue du Port, weeping. That was the day when the final evacuation of Dunkerque was announced. Colonel Merle had the forbidding look of an old bulldog and an assertive walk that belied the meaning of his name—"blackbird." To see him cry was frightening. Sitting in my cache, I too gave myself to uncontrolled weeping. We were about to enter, not a period of summer pleasures, but an unknown, menacing existence.

I remember this period of my childhood in greater detail than any other. The good weather came early that year. The plum trees in our garden traded their white blossoms for bright green *reine-claudes*. It was only April: we were still going to school, but it was so warm that we could go swimming. That spring and summer merged into one lengthy outing at the beach. Despite its name, the "lightning war" went on and on. Anguish about my father and my uncles induced a state of suspense that in retrospect, in my memory, has the colors of summertime. The *guerre éclair* was airy, luminous; it smelled of the seashore.

Letters continued to arrive from my father and my grandmother, but those from my uncles at the front stopped. My father wrote that he was about to be drafted; he had been summoned to a medical examination. My grandmother's letters described vividly the "happy little commune" formed by herself and the Rittonis—Clara Rittoni and her son Paul. The three of them were now sharing a small apartment in a working-class section of Paris. There were frequent air raids over the capital; in the middle of the night, wrapped in blankets, they would go down into the cellar of their building, yet they remained in good spirits. Their life was full of camaraderie. Young Paul was their mascot. He was an exceptionally brilliant boy, and my grandmother could not wait to have André and myself become acquainted with him.

On Easter Day, on our round dining table there were eggs painted the true colors of Easter—pink, green, purple. This was before food coloring disappeared, and we had to use onionskins to dye eggs. The Chernushkis were pouring tea when a boy and a big woman carrying two suitcases walked into our dining room. Paul Rittoni and an emissary of my grandmother had just arrived in Saint-Denis on the afternoon bus.

Solemnly, the woman handed the Chernushkis a letter, which they read aloud. Paul no longer could stand the air raids over Paris; my grandmother asked her daughters to take him in as a member of our family. André and I were full of joy as we offered colored eggs to the newcomers. Once again my grandmother had come up with a miracle—a new friend for us.

While the Chernushkis served tea to Paul's companion, who would be going back to Paris at dawn the next day, André led Paul to the room he shared with his mother and little Kiska. He showed him his toy soldiers—the miniature old-fashioned kind made of wafer-thin lead—and his roller skates. Then he took him on a tour of some of the Maison Ardeber's wonders—which, until that day, had been *ours*, his and mine. He showed him the corner closet next to Ariadne's room with the black tricorn admiral's hat on its highest shelf, and the collection of leatherbound *Illustrations,* going back to the 1850s. That night, Paul was to share André's bed. The boys were going to sleep in what we called "playing card formation," head to toe. I was excluded. With a heavy heart, I went up to bed in my mother's room.

The next morning Natasha and Ariadne went to call on Mademoiselle Charles. A little refugee from Paris had arrived in our midst. Would Mademoiselle Charles put another room at our disposal? Since the salon, a repository of Ardeber treasures, could not be opened, what about Dr. Ardeber's study beyond our kitchen?

Mademoiselle Charles told my aunts that she had to consult

Monsieur le Curé about this new conflict between her Christian duties and Dr. Ardeber's earthly interests. In the middle of the afternoon she arrived carrying a ring full of enormous keys. She had decided to let the *petit refugié* stay in her cousin's study.

She tried to open the small door connecting our kitchen to the new room, but the rusty lock resisted. Finally, Natasha was able to give the key a creaky turn. In the dark, the wooden shutters were unhooked and pushed open. The room was tiny, it smelled of mustiness, but its French doors opened into the springtime garden. The study contained a tall walnut writing desk and a sofa. Paul would sleep on the sofa, while André's own bed, a folding cot, was to be brought down from his mother's room.

Before leaving, Mademoiselle Charles took another, smaller bunch of keys out of her pocket. After several attempts to match one to the lock of the upper section of the desk she succeeded—and we were stunned. Inside, on a shelf next to several medical folios, there was a glass jar. It contained an enormous coiled snake floating in a yellowish liquid. Mademoiselle Charles quickly slammed the door shut. The fact that there was a pickled snake in that otherwise desirable room eased my regrets about not living in it.

While the boys were moving in, I climbed on the "thinking wall" and examined the situation created by Paul's intrusion into our life. Since infancy I had shared everything with André. For the sake of his friendship I had been happy to partake in whatever "manly" pastimes he had proposed—climbing trees, exploring rooftops. But now André, who had always been shy of outsiders, would no longer need me—he had a new friend. I felt very lonely.

As days went by, it became more obvious that André was

delighted with Paul. He did not seem to notice certain traits that at times made his new friend a bit ridiculous—but then I was not above looking for weaknesses in Paul. For example, it seemed to me that he was rather cowardly. On his first day among us he had refused to follow André onto the roofs of the Maison Ardeber, and he never changed his mind about this. To my satisfaction, studying the Charles domain from above remained the illicit pleasure that only André and I indulged in.

An only child brought up by a mother whom he adored, Paul told enthralling stories about Clara. All sorts of important people were constantly asking his mother to marry them, but she preferred to devote herself fully to her son and to certain high causes. In Spain she had played a crucial part in the defense of Barcelona against the Franquists. Paul himself, carrying a red banner, had marched on the Champs Elysées during a gigantic anti-Fascist demonstration. He showed us a red kerchief he had worn on that day over a regulation khaki shirt, which looked quite military.

Paul Rittoni was bigger than André and myself, yet at the same time he looked babyish because of his plumpness. He was handsome, blue-eyed, not without a faint resemblance to Mussolini, or so it seemed to me: he had a straight nose and a strong lower jaw. I did not know it, but his good looks were to come into fashion, irresistibly, only a few months later—those of the healthy, blond Aryan male.

My grandmother and Clara Rittoni reached Saint-Denis in the middle of May, just before all hope of holding the French front lines dismantled by the German armored panzer divisions had faded. A dizzying, lengthy vacation started for us on Oléron. My mother and aunts, overjoyed to have their mother with them, received Clara as a close friend. As usual after a trip, my grandmother had presents for everyone. For André and myself, she brought Alexandre Dumas's *The Three Musketeers*. She also brought news: she had seen my father on the eve of her departure from Paris. He was to be enrolled in the French army by July.

A delegation of young Chernushkis again called on Mademoiselle Charles. We were now a genuine *famille nombreuse*—there were five women and six children under our roof. Events were taking a tragic turn for France. Our landlady was patriotic; her fiancé, it was said, had been killed at Verdun. She agreed, without any preliminary talks with her confessor, to open the Ardebers' salon for my grandmother's and Clara's use.

Paul, André, and I carried to the safety of Mademoiselle Charles's own house certain intricately shaped vases, side tables, and embroidered screens. I was sorry to see them disappear: these things were useless, but they made the salon look like a palace out of *The Three Musketeers*. Then we helped my grandmother and Clara move in. We picked flowers for the lesser vases left on the mantel; the beds were made up with heavy linen sheets provided by Mademoiselle Charles. Suitcases were unpacked.

The "grand salon" of the Maison Ardeber was a sumptuous room. It was spacious enough for a pair of mahogany double beds, which looked like huge boats, and for two armoires facing each other across the room. One of them was a traditional French *armoire à glace*. It had the only full-length mirror in the house, and I loved to look at myself in it, especially as I saw myself reflected against a background of clustered pink blossoms and green leaves—the chestnut tree in our garden was in bloom. If one opened the mirrored doors of the armoire simultaneously and very slowly, a double cascade of luminous spots burst in and spun around the room in a joyful collision.

As for the second armoire, it was huge, of light wood decorated with beautiful eighteenth-century carvings. Our landlady said that it had to be left locked. It was valuable in itself, and so were its contents—so much so that, when her cousin the doctor was leaving for North Africa, he had carried off the armoire key with him. Mademoiselle Charles did not tell us what was inside the armoire. Perhaps she did not know. We took for granted its majestic presence. We did not suspect the danger it contained.

I spent a lot of time in the salon visiting with my grandmother and with Clara. I sat quietly as they chatted while getting dressed and putting on their makeup. They talked about Parisian friends, about their life in the "happy little commune." Against our country setting, Clara was a figure of refinement. She had carefully set golden blond hair and white, well-manicured hands, with nails painted a pale pink. She was tender: she often took me on her lap and called me *ma chérie*.

Clara told us about her adventures during the siege of Barcelona. She had cared for the wounded on the battlefield. Once she took out of the *armoire à glace* a khaki garment and put it on. It was a tight-fitting woolen overall, the uniform of the Spanish Republic's women's auxiliary. Worn with a perky peaked military cap, it was very becoming to Clara.

There was an argument behind the adults' backs as to whether Clara's hair was golden naturally or bleached. André, who was always interested in getting to the truth of things, said that it had to be bleached to be so shiny. When he heard this, Paul turned crimson. This was a lie, his mother was a natural blond. It seemed silly that Paul should be so sensitive: who cared whether Clara's hair was bleached or not? The point was that she was a beauty, she was luminous, pure. Paul explained that his mother was not really an Italian but a Triestine—that is, she had Austrian origins, and this explained her coloring.

Our family had known Clara very slightly before the war. She had been a protégée of the Modiglianis, an influential Italian socialist clan whom my grandmother knew even before the Revolution. I had understood from the adults' conversations that Clara had been married to an Italian anarchist named Veniero Spinelli. Veniero had often visited in our house in Le Plessis, but always without Clara. I remembered him as a handsome bearded young man with warm black eyes who liked to bounce children and throw them high up in the air. In a heavily accented, resounding French, Veniero had spoken about the Spanish Republic, and his tirades sounded like poetry. He had fought in Spain in an anarchist battalion.

Once as I started to ask our guest about "her husband Veniero," my grandmother took me aside. I was being tactless. Poor Clara was now separated from Veniero Spinelli. Nor had she ever been married to him officially because Veniero, an anarchist, did not believe in legal marriage. He had deserted Clara, leaving her alone with Paul, and plunging her into despair. This was why my grandmother had decided to share a flat with her and Paul at the beginning of the "phony war."

My grandmother went on to explain that in a small village like Saint-Denis, the fact that Clara had never been officially married would seem shocking if it became known. If someone was to ask me where Clara's husband was, the answer had to be that Madame Rittoni had been divorced a long time before, without any other explanation. My grandmother had a talk on this subject with André also, but he and I did not discuss the matter. Tacitly, we agreed that it was best not to talk about this secret even between ourselves.

Summer Visitors

The French government had fled to Bordeaux in disarray. Paris, declared an open city, was taken by the Germans on June 13, and Hitler fulfilled his wish: he toured the City of Lights, now his own, on a radiant June morning. But Saint-Denis remained serene. Its white houses shimmered in the sun, and the ocean was a deep blue. I remember the heat, and a succession of picnics on Côte Sauvage. At that time, being away from the village distracted the Chernushkis. The immense, empty beach seemed to proclaim that whatever was happening in the rest of the world could only be a bad dream.

The one event that made war real in Saint-Denis was the arrival, late one morning, of two buses on Place du Marché. They were filled with refugees who stepped out hesitantly, one at a time, into the hot glare of the graveled Place. These people were from Alsace, six or seven families, including grandparents, parents, and many small children. The refugees were darkhaired and wore heavy winter clothes. They looked exhausted.

ISLAND IN TIME

Monsieur Guyonnet, the schoolmaster, took them inside the school, which stood empty since classes had been called off in May. There they were served an improvised lunch.

That afternoon, the mayor of Saint-Denis and his council held an extraordinary meeting. The refugees were assigned quarters *chez l'habitant*—in the houses of people who normally took in vacationers in the summer. After a few days everyone in Saint-Denis forgot that the Alsatians were refugees; the weariness in their eyes faded; they looked like ordinary vacationers as they shopped for freshly baked bread in the mornings and went to the beach with their children in the afternoons.

For us on Oléron, the other event of these days was General de Gaulle's broadcast from London on June 18. Mademoiselle Charles had found out that this obscure, recently promoted general had reached London and was going to address the French nation. Perhaps he would give some guidance for the future. Mademoiselle Charles asked the Chernushkis to listen to the radio with her, and my grandmother took me along.

I remember more clearly our landlady's salon with its torn satin drapes and the shadowy corridors leading to it than I do the words of the man who was able to become, through singular inspiration, the incarnation of all that was patriotic in France in 1940. Yet, as the years went on, as the Germans seemed destined to conquer the world, his speech was to become a manifesto. Its text would be circulated in secret. I was to learn it by heart:

> Is the last word said?
> Must hope disappear?
> Is our defeat final?
> No!

> Notwithstanding all our faults, our procrastination, our sufferings, the means to destroy our enemy do exist in this world. Stricken today by his mechanical might, we will conquer with a superior force. This will be the world's fate.
>
> No matter what happens, the flame of French resistance will not go out.

The day before, on June 17, Pétain, the new leader of the French government—an octogenarian, a Marshal of France, the hero of Verdun—had proclaimed that France had lost the war. The time for an armistice had come. In slightly rasping accents, he had said at last what many in France had secretly wanted to hear since those clear September days the year before: it was all right to bow to Hitler. The tone was set for years to come:

> ... certain of the trust of the whole people, I make the gift of my person to France, to attenuate its misfortune. With a heavy heart I say today that we must cease to fight.

Comforting as this message was, it was misleading. The armistice between France and Germany was not signed until June 22. Many French soldiers took the expression "we must cease to fight" at face value and dropped their weapons on June 17. This made it possible for the Germans to seize huge numbers of prisoners in the course of the following week.

Suddenly the French were divided. The great majority

would follow the voice of reason as expressed by the venerable Pétain. A very few others thought, like de Gaulle, that France had lost the battle of France but the war was not over. Our family was in this group. Under the leadership of Churchill, England would be able to continue the war. Sooner or later, America would throw her force behind it. The war was only beginning.

A couple of days after General de Gaulle's appeal, returning home at noon from the beach, I saw my father's bicycle from a distance. It stood against the low wall of our garden. I recognized it at once. It was a pale green and had racing handlebars. Near it stood three women's bicycles. They were clumsy and black, with oversized suitcases tied to their racks.

I do not think that I have ever been happier in my life than at that moment, running toward my father's bicycle along a rue du Port that shimmered in the white midday heat. I rushed into our garden and into the house. Surrounded by the Chernushkis, my father was drinking tea in the dining room. There were three strangers in the room with him, a man and two women, also drinking tea. Joyfully, the Chernushkis were racing between the kitchen and the dining room. They were making sandwiches. Everyone was speaking at once, and the little boys were dancing in circles with triumphant cries. I gathered that the strangers were the Fedotovs, parents and daughter. They had just arrived from Paris with my father.

The Fedotovs were acquaintances of our family. Pyotr Georgevich Fedotov was an eminent theologian—I did not know what a theologian was, but I guessed that it was someone rather like a priest. And, indeed, everything about Pyotr

Georgevich was vaguely ecclesiastical. Small and slender, he wore a wispy goatee. He had unbelievably soft hands—I realized this as I was made to shake hands with the new arrivals.

The two Fedotov ladies, mother and daughter, were as tall and strong as Mr. Fedotov was delicate. Madame Fedotov, the mother, was angular and wore a pince-nez looped around her neck with a black cord. Her movements were violent. With her booming voice, she might well have been an incarnation of earthly passions. Her daughter Nina had to be an embodiment of earthly repose. Nina was a statuesque, tranquil blond of twenty-four or twenty-five.

My father had been able to leave Paris because of the Fedotovs, a family influential in Russian Orthodox circles who had been issued a travel permit by the French police ministry. Finding his factory's doors closed on the eve of the German entry into Paris, he had traveled on their pass, although at the time it was against the law for a foreigner to leave his place of work without a permit. Just ahead of the Germans, they had bicycled on roads overflowing with refugees. Near them, people had been machine-gunned by enemy aviators. At night, they had slept in haystacks.

Just before they reached Le Chapus, where the ferry to Oléron originated, they had encountered roadblocks set up by the French gendarmerie. The French authorities were directing the refugees toward the central provinces of France, which were presumed to have better food supplies than the coastal region. "On Oléron, you'll eat stones," a gendarme told my father. They escaped his vigilance only in the evening, when they found a side street that bypassed the roadblock.

Drinking tea, the travelers told us about their trip. They sat for a long time in the coolness of our dining room. Then they took turns washing in the kitchen in a flat oval zinc tub: it was their first bath since they had left Paris. When the midday heat subsided, my grandmother went out to try to find quarters in the village for the Fedotovs. She was able to rent a room on rue de la Muse, but it would not be ready till the following day. The Fedotovs spent their first night in Saint-Denis sleeping on the dining room floor on makeshift bedding.

Mademoiselle Charles dropped by the Maison Ardeber to greet the newcomers. The Fedotovs met with her approval. In their dark clothes they looked respectable despite their harrowing week on the roads of France. Our landlady did become alarmed once, when Madame Fedotov impetuously declared, in a heavily accented, overwrought voice, "I am ready to wash the floors in the butcher's shop—anything to earn our right to stay in Saint-Denis!"

"Dear Madame, calm yourself," Mademoiselle Charles had said in a flustered voice. "That will be unnecessary. All strangers are welcome here at a time like this!"

The following days were spent in catching up with my father's adventures. Wherever we went—to the nearby beaches or to Côte Sauvage on bicycle—I kept asking him to tell me about his trip. It was terrifying, it gave one an intimation of what war was like.

I asked my father to tell me certain episodes of his journey time and again. One had to do with a crazed French officer who had demanded his papers as he was standing in line for bread in a small village in the Loire valley. Finding out that my father was a foreigner, the man had wanted to shoot him on the spot as a spy. My father dashed into the crowd and disappeared. Another episode was the bombardment at Etampes—the roar of the plane engines, entire buildings lifted up into the air, an enormous red glow filling the sky. Then there were the stranded children—hundreds of them walking alone on the highways, having lost their parents in the debacle.

Secretly, I was happy that the armistice had been signed: my father was not going off to war. If only we could be sure that my uncles were alive! The future was dark, yet the rumors circulating in Saint-Denis were surprisingly reassuring. The Germans, credited with so many atrocities during the previous war, were said to be behaving "correctly" toward civilians. France was being divided into two separate zones. The Free Zone was to the south and had a summer spa, Vichy, as its capital. We were in the other, the Occupied Zone, which comprised Paris and the Atlantic and northern provinces. The "lightning war" was over.

Summer days succeeded one another, but no German was to be seen on Oléron. The green plums in our garden had ripened and now tasted like honey. July came, and the Fourteenth of July was marked by a solemn gathering on Place de la Mairie. There, in a special ceremony, the French flag was raised above the door of the Mairie. The inhabitants of Saint-Denis wore their Sunday clothes to the ceremony and Monsieur le Maire made a speech. With a tremor in his voice, the gray-haired, sunburned peasant said that from now on, it would be up to each person in Saint-Denis individually to uphold the French honor. The municipal band, "*la Fanfare Municipale,*" made up of a trumpet, a clarinet, cymbals, and a drum, played a last, brassy "Marseillaise." Several old men standing near us were crying. On that Fourteenth of July in the blue shadow of the centenary elms, I felt a member of our community.

Almost every day people arrived at our house. They were relatives, friends, or friends of friends, and my family received them with their customary warmth. My grandmother had been brought up in a world of unrestricted hospitality. She never minded guests, even when they appeared in huge numbers, and even if they never went home. It was on her invitation, extended when she was still in Paris, that so many people were coming to Saint-Denis. The young Chernushkis were equanimous: once again times were catastrophic, and a show of solidarity was in order.

Like the Fedotovs, our visitors were émigrés fleeing the Germans. They were hoping to proceed south, to Marseilles or Bordeaux; from there, they would sail for America. Some already had their visas, others were waiting for them; it made little difference just then. Having reached Oléron, they could not proceed. For many weeks there had been no transportation whatever in our part of France.

In the afternoons while it was too hot to go out comfortably, our guests drank tea and discussed philosophy and politics in the dining room of the Maison Ardeber. Sometimes my father joined in: he particularly liked Pyotr Georgevich, although they often argued. My father maintained that it was only a matter of time before Hitler and Stalin would clash. Pyotr Georgovich did not agree: in his opinion, the two dictators were incarnations of the Anti-Christ who had come together in a lasting, unholy alliance. He quoted Alexander Blok's poem in which the Scythians—the Russians—challenge Europe. It sounded like some dark prophecy:

> There are millions of you, but our numbers
>   are endless.
> We are the Asians with the slanted eyes.
> Measure yourselves against us, try.
> We are the Scythians, we are the Asians.

> This time we shall not shield you, Europe!
> We shall be watching with our narrow eyes
> The death-brew boil. . . .

Whenever Madame Fedotov participated in these conversations, she quoted the Apocalypse and her comments had the power of generating ever-increasing confusion. Arcane philosophical arguments would be born and become heated disagreements.

From time to time, Julien and his cousin Maurice, the only member of the Desmons family who had reached Oléron that summer, came to spend the afternoon with us. Julien, who had come in one day not knowing that my father had arrived in Saint-Denis, was quite taken by him. At first, he had seemed apprehensive, but the ice was broken between them in the course of a discussion about the relative merits of Russian and French classics—Pushkin versus Racine.

Julien and Maurice pretended to be unaffected by news of the French defeat. They joked about the more colorful visitors at the Maison Ardeber. After hearing the Fedotovs' scary predictions, I liked to listen to their banter. I did not take offense when Julien called our family *la tribu* ("the tribe"). We must indeed have looked exotic against the village setting. The young women dressed like Parisiennes; Madame Fedotov in her floating dark clothes and her pince-nez; my father, the head of the family, who looked like a Georgian prince.

It was Julien who brought the Kalitas into our life. It happened on a hot midafternoon when Clara had come to the beach with us—with Julien and Maurice and *les jeunes*, as she called us, the older children. Soon after we had arrived on

Grande Plage, the more exposed of the three beaches of Saint-Denis, several people emerged from the pines bordering it. They walked clumsily toward the sea in the heavy, shifting sand. Opening up their umbrellas and spreading towels on the sand, they settled near us in a noisy group. André and I became curious: the wind was carrying a mixture of Russian and French conversation.

Spotting Julien, one of the strangers, a gray-haired Frenchman in an old-fashioned striped bathing suit, walked over and greeted him. Julien, in turn, presented Monsieur Martin, a friend of his father, to Clara, and we were all asked to join the Martins and their friends under their beach umbrellas. Clara led the way with Monsieur Martin, followed by Julien, Maurice, and the three of us.

The Martins lived in Paris in the winter and owned an old farmhouse on the road to Méray. They had just arrived on the island after some fearful adventures on the French highways. Monsieur Martin was a lively smiling man. Madame Martin, his wife, was very fat and draped in an enormous terry cloth robe. She was friendly to children. She told me about her daughter Renée, who was two years older than I.

The Martins had with them a party of four White Russians, their summer tenants on route de Méray. In addition to two ladies, two middle-aged sisters clad in fancy beach pyjamas and named Nadetchka and Lizotchka—Julien and Maurice whispered preposterous comments about their clinging outfits—there was a Russian émigré couple, the Kalitas. At once the Kalitas were entranced by Clara—we all noticed this. Julien later maintained that both of them had had a *coup de foudre* that day on the beach, falling in love with her at first sight.

The Kalitas were in their forties, well dressed and prosperous-looking. Andrei Kalita was a stocky man who had a roaring laugh and an exaggeratedly jolly manner. He ran in and out of the surf with a show of athletic prowess. His wife, who did not go swimming, looked older than he and very proper. She had a fussy social manner. At once André and I recognized someone who would pick on children for the pleasure of it. Though Russian, she was of German origin, having been born into the Baltic nobility, she explained to Clara. Vera Kalita held in her lap a fancily clipped, small white terrier named Bebka. Bebka barked loudly whenever anyone went into the water. Like Madame Kalita, Bebka would not go swimming.

This encounter led to more afternoon encounters on Grande Plage between the Kalitas and Clara and Paul. André and I came along—André went everywhere with his new friend, and I followed, although the boys did not always make me feel welcome. But I was smitten with Clara, I liked to be with her. During these afternoons on the beach, Kalita paid playful court to Clara.

As for Madame Kalita, she was extremely taken not only by Clara, but also by Paul. She talked with him as an adult, and she lauded his excellent manners. This momentarily brought André and me together again: to be the object of Madame Kalita's attention would be a misfortune. We were satisfied with the fact that Madame Kalita ignored us except to deplore, once in a great while, in muted tones, how undernourished we looked. Taking Clara aside, she would inquire whether our mothers took sufficiently good care of us. Occasionally, she asked one of us to take Bebka for a stroll along the beach, but that was the extent of her interest in us.

One afternoon, invited by Clara, the Kalitas came to the Maison Ardeber for tea. They seemed unimpressed with our family's ways and with our other Russian visitors, although Madame Kalita made an exception of my grandmother, to whom she deferred. The Kalitas started asking Clara out frequently. In midsummer they left their rooms at the Martins' and moved into a comfortable cottage in the center of the village, near the bakery.

There, according to Clara, the Kalitas enjoyed elegant gardens, which were hidden from passersby by high walls and a solid wooden gate. Several times a week they invited Clara and Paul for afternoon coffee and cakes with various members of the local bourgeoisie whom they had met through the gregarious Martins. One day, Clara was even introduced to Saint-Denis' leading *grande dame*, Madame Bourrade, the mother of Gigi and Roberte.

Clara found Andrei Kalita rather vulgar, but she was impressed with Madame Kalita. And then, the Kalitas were so kind to Paul! They gave him extraordinary presents, such as an electric train procured only Heaven knows how on Oléron at that time. From the beginning, Clara had wanted to become acquainted with more people around Saint-Denis, and now the Kalitas were helpful. "We cannot live here as outcasts," Clara had often said to my grandmother before her meeting with the Martins and the Kalitas. "Let us *do* something about it!"

My grandmother agreed that it would be good to have more friends in Saint-Denis. However, she was not especially drawn to the local bourgeoisie; instead, she was friendly with Madame Braud, a mustachioed old woman across the street who told stories about Oléron, about the way the *vendanges* had once been done, when people crushed the grapes with their feet and danced and drank all night afterwards. Like Clara, I, on the other hand, was intrigued by the beau monde of Saint-Denis. The peasants wore dark clothes. They were severe, they intimidated me—they never smiled at children.

More than anything in the world I wanted to meet the Bourrade girls who rode their bicycles down rue du Port in sparkling white tennis clothes. The fact that Julien pronounced them mindless did not make them seem less attractive. However, I had to content myself with Renée, the Martins' daughter, who had taken me under her wing. She invited me to play in the walled-in garden of her parents' farmhouse. There we picked midsummer figs or skipped rope. I found Renée, an outgoing, plump blond of about thirteen, predictable, but I liked to go to places beyond the world of the Maison Ardeber. There was something intoxicating in the social swirl that had overtaken our life, and like my grandmother, I loved it.

One July evening, Victor Chernov, my adoptive grandfather, and his second wife, Ida Samoylovna, walked into our garden. The small boys had already had their supper, and the Chernushkis were setting the table in the dining room for the rest of the family, for nine—we were a large household.

Ida Samoylovna had been a part of my childhood fantasies, and it seemed quite natural that she would put in an appearance during that phantasmagoric summer. She was a former Bolshevik once befriended by my grandmother. She had caused Victor Chernov to leave his family in the early twenties.

Ida, seeming lost and helpless, had implanted herself in the midst of the Chernovs in 1917 upon their return to Russia. She appealed to my grandmother's sense of compassion time and time again. Probably she had been aware of the fact that Victor Chernov was at that moment one of the important political personalities in Russia.

Now Ida, this mythical creature, was sitting on the garden bench by our yucca. I had not expected a fabled archvillain to look so much like one. Ida resembled a big gargoyle. She was puffed up by arthritis, the hands lying in her lap resembled fleshy claws with a life of their own. It seemed astonishing that anyone would have wanted to leave my pretty grandmother for this woman.

When the Chernovs appeared in the garden, my grandmother had been at first seized with panic. What would become of her reputation if a *second* Madame Chernov settled in the village, she asked in an emotional manner, and she took refuge in her room, then came out and said that if the Chernovs were going to live in Saint-Denis, she would leave the island. She would walk to Paris if there was no other way to get there. Little by little, as she listened to her daughters, she calmed down.

Soon her natural kindness returned, and she was taking a cup of tea to Ida in the garden.

The new arrivals explained that they were headed for the United States. They were hoping to leave for Marseilles as soon as possible. But, of course, they found themselves stranded on Saint-Denis for several weeks.

During that time, Victor Chernov came to the Maison Ardeber often. He was a portly, smiling man with a neatly trimmed white beard whom André and I had remembered liking from his rare visits to Le Plessis. He loved children, and he was said to have been a wonderful companion to the young Chernushkis when they were small. Now he played checkers with André, and he sang mellow Russian folksongs for the small boys—he had a rich, smooth, bass voice. Yet everything about him seemed subdued. Obsessively he discussed how to leave for the United States as soon as possible. Fear, the strong, persistent kind, was something I had never observed before.

My recollection of my father's favorite lines out of Pasternak dates to that time. I remember him reciting them to me as we were gathering driftwood on the beach one afternoon:

> The tales of our fathers are like the
>   reigns of the Stuarts,
> Farther away than Pushkin, they can
>   only be seen in a dream.

In those years when we read so many historical romances, "the reigns of the Stuarts" seemed less dreamlike than our life on Oléron. Yet our summer visitors were not dream figures. Our past, Europe's past, had created our present, my father said as we talked on the beach. Everything everyone did had a meaning, it was what shaped the world. Nor was I to mind the fact that I was a girl. Girls often lacked willpower, but if I had the desire to do something, and the will, I could do, or be, whatever I wished. The main thing was not to be afraid.

My father seemed certain of this, and I believed him.

Flags and Smiles

Fear, still elusive and hard to recognize in its disguise of flags and smiles, entered our lives on a clear July day. The Germans marched into Saint-Denis on July 20. The evening before, at twilight, the town crier had made his rounds, reading out an announcement by Monsieur le Maire. The civilian population was to abstain from any hostile demonstration against the Occupation armies arriving in Saint-Denis the next day. People were ordered not to leave their houses until a further announcement by the mayor.

The weather that day was marvelous, though rather windy—I recall thinking about the big, white-crowned waves breaking on Grande Plage. But like all the other inhabitants of Saint-Denis who spent the day peering from behind drawn curtains or closed shutters, we had to follow the Germans' slow, clanking takeover of Saint-Denis from indoors. We watched out of my grandmother's French window, while the little boys looked out of the window of Natasha's room above it. It was a favorite observation post whenever they were not allowed in the garden. From there, on winter Sundays after Mass, they had studied the traditional stroll of the inhabitants of Saint-Denis: from the church to our jetty and back, regardless of the weather. What they were witnessing now was another kind of spectacle—they were transfixed.

A German unit of several hundred men was moving into our village. These men had traveled a long way to our island, and at last they had reached their goal: only the ocean lay beyond rue du Port. Despite its empty streets, Saint-Denis in the sunshine must have appeared inviting. The soldiers were coming to the seaside for a holiday, a prelude to their victory celebration.

The Germans were briskly marching toward the Hotel Gai Soleil two blocks below us on rue du Port. They were to be quartered in that sprawling establishment, which had been boarded up since the beginning of the war. Six or seven formations of twenty young men each walked by, singing with great gusto a particularly mindless marching song:

> *Halli, hallo, halli, hallo,*
> *Halli, hallo, halli, hallo,*
> *Halli, hallo, ho ho ho ho,*
> *Hallo ho ho, ho ho, ho ho. . . .*

They wore gray green uniforms and black leather boots. The weapons they carried—pistols, rifles, and submachine guns—were also black and freshly oiled and polished. All were tall, blond, and very young. They had been preceded by a dozen men on motorcycles who wore steel helmets, with submachine guns slung at their sides—a thundering detachment that had made the windowpanes vibrate and sing.

The units on foot were followed by a dozen slow-moving trucks that were filled with soldiers who were a little older than the singing young men. Behind the trucks came heavy black cannons on wheels dragged by teams of horses. This parade, which lasted an hour, was closed by another detachment of motorcyclists rushing by like noisy, helmeted devils.

Everything about the Germans was black and gray green, even the camouflaged cloths on their chariots, which looked like black and green zebra skins. The street had filled with dust and the smells of leather, gasoline, and horse manure. This powerful new odor floated into the house and lingered. Even before the dust had settled, several black autos roared past our house. Incessant coming and going along the street: soldiers were rushing to and from the Mairie.

At dusk, the town crier read out the first of what were to be the innumerable German decrees regulating our new life. Curfew in Saint-Denis was between 9:00 P.M. and 6:00 A.M. Anyone seen out of doors between these hours would be shot without warning by German patrols. The civilian population was reminded that it had nothing to fear from the Germans if it obeyed all regulations and behaved in a disciplined manner.

The Germans spilled over on both sides of rue du Port, well beyond the Hotel Gai Soleil, with its wooden bungalows and small dance hall. Every day they requisitioned new buildings as lodgings and stables. There were many unused barns and empty summer houses around Saint-Denis, whose owners had not reached Oléron that year.

Once the Germans had moved into a house it was

impossible to evict them, even if the owners appeared in person. Enterprising and ever anxious to improve their comforts, the soldiers started to move furniture from one villa to another. Looting was said to be strictly forbidden, but certain officers did have suspicious-looking crates packed up in their gardens.

The villas hidden in the greenery on both sides of rue du Port below us appealed to the Germans. They were the embodiment of some modest French family's life dream. Certain people in Saint-Denis, like the Martins and our neighbor Colonel Merle, who had been Oléronais for several generations, lovingly continued to maintain their old farms as summer houses. No less lovingly, newcomers had built cottages along the beach. Above their entrance doors enameled plaques edged with sprigs of mimosa or bunches of pansies announced that these were Villa Mon Désir, Villa Mon Rêve.

The soldiers could be seen running up and down rue du Port, waving the universal symbols of house-cleaning: mop, feather duster, and the pretzel-shaped wicker contraption on a handle that was used to beat rugs. They scurried in the sunshine, trading bedding and hanging curtains. Inside and out they were decorating the walls of their houses with portraits of Hitler and with Nazi slogans in carefully lettered Gothic characters written out on red cloth or painted directly on the walls.

The German dining mess was located in Hotel Gai Soleil, and the smell of warm food drifted up toward our house. The hotel was now decorated with a profusion of Nazi flags, its picture windows lined with neatly potted, even-sized red geraniums in full bloom. Where had the Germans procured them? Certainly not around Saint-Denis. The inhabitants of our village, like islanders all over the world, were fond of exotic plants, the kind that had once been brought back to Oléron by sailors from distant lands. These were carefully tended, divided, and shared with neighbors. They grew in odd containers, not in expensive, new clay pots. "They look so common, these fat red geraniums," Renée Martin said once as we walked past the Gai Soleil. Otherwise she ignored the Germans and their activities: We never discussed the war, she and I, although my parents said that the Martins were probably pro-British rather than pro-German.

Soon after their arrival, the Germans hired one of the refugees from Alsace to serve as an interpreter between themselves and the French authorities. She was a young woman, eighteen or nineteen, called Rose. Her family was Jewish. Most of the Alsatians who had arrived on Oléron in that party were Jews.

For their Kommandantur ("headquarters") the Germans had requisitioned the only fancy villa near the Mairie, Villa Adrienne, which was said to have a telephone and indoor toilets. It looked vaguely like an elongated version of an alpine chalet, with its wooden balconies and roof overhang painted bright blue.

German motorcyclists came up to the Villa Adrienne, and their engines' backfiring made the chickens in the neighborhood squawk wildly. Couriers on bikes were leaving from the villa's iron gates. An occasional black automobile drove up to the gate, and Germans of high military rank emerged and walked into the villa and out again with clipped, resounding steps. The dry clattering of typewriters filled the air.

The German commandant of Saint-Denis, Colonel Schmidt, was said to be "very correct, very decent" by some members of the community who demonstrated their sympathy for the Germans by praising them in places where they could be overheard—after church, in stores. These included Monsieur le Curé, and the Bourrades. We did not know anyone in this group, soon referred to as *"les collaborateurs,"* but what they had to say was reported to the Chernushkis whenever they went shopping in the village.

As for Clara, after the Germans' arrival in the village, she had refused to go out altogether. She was deeply distressed: "The Germans look at me with suspicion as if they knew that I am an anti-Fascist," she said. However, the Germans' attitude toward the civilians could not have been more friendly, and eventually Clara started to go out again. She continued to see the Kalitas. Through them she learned what went on among the German officers stationed in Saint-Denis—what ranks they had and the reputations they enjoyed among their fellow officers.

At that time we lived on rumors. After her visits with the Kalitas, Clara reported extraordinary ones regarding the current military events—about secret negotiations between Britain and Germany, about the United States' readiness to enter the war on Germany's side. The Kalitas, who spoke German, had acquaintances among the more civilized officers stationed around Saint-Denis. Many in Saint-Denis had reservations about the Kalitas, but Clara maintained that they could not be *collaborateurs*. Rather, they were ordinary White Russians.

On the very first Sunday after the Germans' arrival, Monsieur le Curé had made an impassioned sermon against the British: God was on the German side, the just side. Soon afterward, speaking with my grandmother on the street, Mademoiselle Charles bluntly said that she was appalled by our curé, who had come to Saint-Denis not long before. The previous curé had retired because of old age, but, fortunately, he still was her confessor. For a long time, our landlady had controlled many church activities, dictating the manner in which the church was decorated on holidays and who was to be a choir boy. The curé had at first humored her, but new winds were now blowing in Saint-Denis. The red-faced, tough-looking curé, who rode a woman's big black bicycle and warmly welcomed German soldiers to our church, felt that Mademoiselle Charles belonged to the past.

In August, two letters arrived within a few days of each other: both my uncles were alive. Ariadne was succinctly informed that Volodia, who had been seriously wounded, was on his way to a camp in an undetermined part of Germany. He had been made a prisoner of war. The French government had awarded him the croix de guerre for high military deeds. Several months later, Ariadne started a correspondence with my uncle by means of rare, officially printed postcards. Eventually, she was allowed to send regular letters and an occasional package of clothing and foodstuffs to the stalag where he was imprisoned: Volodia and his campmates were employed in the construction of the first German autobahn near Potsdam.

As for Daniel, he had been demobilized and was now recuperating in a hospital near Biarritz in the Free Zone. In June, in Alsace, he had been wounded. For days, with a group of survivors from a violent battle near the town of Soissons, he had wandered westward, escaping German encirclement. Daniel was shot in the leg while picking cherries in an isolated orchard. By then, he and his companions were terribly hungry: they did not dare go into the villages for fear of being captured by the Germans.

Daniel had had the good fortune of being helped by a

group of French nuns, who put him on a military hospital train headed southward, toward what was to become the Free Zone. He was planning to return to Paris to look for a job and would try to send us money soon.

Indeed, we were getting desperate for money. My father was looking for a job around Saint-Denis, but although there was a huge amount of farm work to be done, the peasants were reluctant to hire a Parisian. "Parisians don't know how to work," they said to my father with friendly grins, offering him a glass of wine as he called on them. Everyone on the island was persuaded that the good *Maréchal* was going to bring the war prisoners back in time for the *vendanges*.

Daniel had decided to let Natasha and their boys stay on with us in Saint-Denis: life in Paris was said to be extremely difficult.

Little by little, our new life under the Occupation began to acquire a rhythm of its own. Almost every evening at twilight the town crier bicycled from street corner to street corner. Beating a drum roll, he read out ordinances issued by the German authorities. These were very long and detailed—the Germans left nothing to chance. The use of boats and autos was forbidden to the civilians. So was traveling to the mainland, which could be done only in case of serious emergency, on a laissez-passer delivered by the Kommandantur. For Oléron was situated within the coastal zone that was to be fortified in preparation for a decisive confrontation with England.

The ordinances touching on our daily lives often sounded sinister. A strict curfew was maintained. There was an absolute interdiction against listening to British radio broadcasts—anyone caught was to be turned over to the gestapo. However, in Saint-Denis the Germans abstained from issuing humiliating regulations; in Saint-Pierre they were said to have forbidden the peasants to carry rabbits by the ears and chickens by the legs—they considered this barbarous.

To the islanders' delight, the Germans seemed to have unlimited supplies of French money. Within the first week of their arrival they had purchased the whole stock of the souvenir shop near us. Gone were the toy sailboats and the postcards. The stores of Saint-Denis stood empty, and bread at the bakery was sold out by ten o'clock in the morning. However, no one on Oléron was worried. Fresh vegetables and fruit were still plentiful.

The Germans started acquiring extraordinary quantities of wine and cognac directly from the inhabitants. These transactions, which left both parties highly satisfied, were conducted mostly in sign language laced with French and German baby talk. The peasants who sold their wine to the Germans maintained that they were doing this "to demoralize them." On Sunday afternoons, soldiers could be seen meandering unsteadily up and down rue du Port. The little boys, sitting on their wall, watched in fascination. The soldiers were sometimes accompanied by young women. There were a half-dozen of them who became notorious. In the village they were referred to contemptuously as *les horizontales*.

One afternoon my grandmother took Clara to Méray to introduce her to Madame Duval and Madame Lutin. At the last minute, when it became clear that Paul was not going with them, she agreed to take me along. To go anywhere with Clara was exciting—and, of course, I was ardently hoping that Julien might be at home. That day there was a crystalline quality to the air, as if summer were at last ending. But, when we looked at the grapes in the vineyards on each side of the road, as my grandmother and I had done the year before, we discovered that they were still hard, like bright green jewels.

My grandmother and Clara were discussing the Chernushkis' plan to hire themselves out for the *vendanges*. They were looking for employers who would pay them in potatoes and wheat. The gendarme's prediction to my father was coming true: "On Oléron, you'll eat stones." From one day to the next, it was becoming impossible to buy foodstuffs on the island. Fortunately, my father had already been hired for the forthcoming *vendanges* by the Michaux family, from Les Huttes, a tiny hamlet at the edge of Côte Sauvage. Michaux had agreed to pay him half in cash and half in potatoes and give him two bottles of wine for each day of work.

This was an ancient tradition on Oléron: everyone on the island, regardless of profession or social status, cut grapes during the *vendanges*. The Oléronais who did not own vineyards went to work for relatives. Few people wanted money: wine, cognac, and lard were the most desirable rewards. Above all, the grape harvest was regarded as the culmination of a year of hard work. Pigs were slaughtered then, and friends gathered for long meals. It was the one festivity of the year on Oléron.

Clara was explaining to my grandmother that to her great disappointment she could not harvest grapes: she reacted badly to too much sun, yet she, too, was worried about money. My grandmother assured her that we were her family and that, as long as we had anything, she and Paul would have their share. Clara said that she had always earned her own living. She was determined to find a secretarial job on the island. Failing this, she would join her friends, the Modiglianis, in Toulouse in the Free Zone. With her customary insistence, my grandmother was arguing that Saint-Denis, small and out of the way, was safer for Clara and little Paul than Toulouse. Big cities would starve first.

And then all of a sudden Clara was telling my grandmother about the Austrian officer she had encountered the day before on the beach. The man had been a distinguished lawyer in Vienna. Because of his education, he had been made an officer in the German army. When the Austrian first had approached her, as she was sunning herself near the jetty, Clara had declined to talk to him. However she had sensed that this man who was speaking with an Austrian accent was a civilized human being. He had exquisite manners. They had ended up by having a conversation.

The officer told Clara that it was only a matter of weeks before England's surrender. A new political order would then triumph in Europe; only the positive aspects of nazism would be retained—social discipline, love of family. Even the Russian allies would mellow under the civilizing influence of this new order. Clara had been impressed by his arguments. Now she wanted to know what my grandmother, a fellow socialist, might think of them.

I was astonished to hear that Clara would have had a conversation with a man in a German uniform. No one in our family would do that, I assumed. I had seen the Chernushkis hurry away, as Germans started patting the little boys on the head or tried to give them chocolate while engaging them in conversation. I saw that my grandmother too was surprised, but then Clara said something about being a Triestine and, therefore, at least part Austrian. How could she have turned her back on a compatriot?

My grandmother paid the greatest attention to Clara's

explanations about the Austrian's vision of the future. She listened with a mixture of bewilderment and eagerness. Anxious to hide her doubts, lest they offend Clara, she asked her whether the officer had said anything about the political climate in Austria. Was it true that they were arresting Jews there for no other reason than that they were Jews? But the officer had said nothing about the current events in his country, he had only discussed its future.

The weather was spoiling as we reached Méray. Black clouds were racing straight at us from the south. It began to rain as we walked through the Lutins' gate. And Julien and Maurice were not at home—they had left for the beach moments before.

Sadness filled the Lutins' house on that afternoon: Madame Duval was ill. Clearly, the Lutins were deeply affected by France's military defeat, although they tried not to show it.

Madame Lutin did not make any of her usual sarcastic remarks about the Oléronais. As for Maître Lutin, he saw a lesson to be learned from the event. Defeat had been caused by lack of discipline on the part of Frenchmen who had gotten used to leading pleasure-seeking lives. Perhaps the Germans would now teach them a sense of order.

I was happy to take refuge in the library. We had brought with us the books that Julien had lent us, and I now selected others to take back. The library was quiet and cool. I felt close to Julien there. I was choosing books with care, running my finger along the shelf of Julien's books of poetry. They were white paperbacks in tantalizing cellophane wrappers. He was lending them to me one by one—I was slowly becoming acquainted with Baudelaire, Verlaine, and the enigmatic Mallarmé. However, in his absence I was reluctant to borrow them. Instead, turning to Madame Duval's shelves I took the plays of Molière in a beautiful old edition. Then my grandmother was calling me; it was time for us to go. Until the last moment, I had hoped that Julien and his cousin might come back from the beach, driven home by the rain. I had listened for their voices, but they had not returned.

Before leaving, my grandmother and I went upstairs to have a few words with Madame Duval. The shutters in her bedroom were closed. She looked very small in her dark mahogany bed. As she talked to my grandmother about the war, she suddenly started to cry. She said, "When the Germans entered Paris, for the first time in my life I was glad that Monsieur Duval was dead."

As we left I had a heavy heart. Madame Duval seemed quite ill. Nor had the visit been a success for Clara. She had not liked the Lutins. "They are nice enough, but they smell of mothballs," was her only comment about them.

On our way home we witnessed one of Oléron's great sunsets. The sky was violet with fantastically shaped clouds piled up high behind the lighthouse at Chassiron. And then a strange thing happened. As we walked, I took Clara's arm as I had done on our way to Méray, but she pulled away from me abruptly, as if she were angry with me. Yet, hard as I thought, I could not remember doing anything that might have offended her. I was surprised and hurt. Later, I took my grandmother's hand in mine and this made me feel better, but I could not forget Clara's gesture. I could not understand it.

Church and State in Saint-Denis

Saint-Denis had several distinct sections, known as *quartiers,* each with its own function and style. On Place de la Mairie, the Mairie and the school faced each other. This was the distinguished part of town where the bourgeoisie lived in solid, two-storied houses, their wooden shutters perpetually half-closed against dust and intrusions. Their monumental doors had brass knockers shaped like a ravishing woman's hand with a ring on her finger and a bracelet on her wrist. Then, there were the strange little figures of cast iron sealed into their walls. They served as hooks when the shutters were open, securing them against the wall. One kind was shaped like the head of a lady in a Renaissance hairdress, another was a man with a pointed beard. Yet another, wearing a beret, looked like Garibaldi. We were told who Garibaldi was—but this made it only all the more bewildering; why should a famous Italian revolutionary in a beret be used to anchor shutters to the walls of houses?

The main street of the peasant section of the village, rue de la Muse, smelled of cow manure. One could spend hours exploring this settlement dating back to the Middle Ages; it both repelled and fascinated us. The peasants' houses were huddled there, low, whitewashed structures with blank walls to the street. Chickens, an enterprising, hardy species on Oléron, ran loose in courtyards and into rue de la Muse. Dogs were chained, two or three for each household, of indescribable races and shapes, sleeping in small wooden doghouses. There was a pig in each courtyard, living on household scraps in a semi-covered pen next to the privy. Every building in town, regardless of its size or purpose, was roofed with beautiful, sun-bleached Roman tiles. Even the wingless stone mills on the village outskirts had their peaked roofs intricately laid out with pale pink tiles.

Every Sunday Mademoiselle Charles and a half-dozen devout churchgoers in shiny black straw hats lingered on Place de la Mairie for long whispered exchanges. Full of self-importance, the majestic curé walked by and nodded, a portly man with a hard, brick-colored face. Civic ceremonies had been held there before the Germans came to Saint-Denis. Now the French flag had been removed from the front of the Mairie, behind which stood our school.

A small engraved stone above the school door proclaimed that it had been dedicated in 1884, like thousands of other schools throughout the French countryside. Under the tenacious anticlerical leadership of President Jules Ferry, France had built its first public schools in defiance of the Catholic church, which had, until then, dominated French education. Indeed, the school of Saint-Denis was a model of rational design. Its four spacious square classrooms opened directly onto a graveled courtyard planted with neatly trimmed, rounded lindens. The yard was divided in two by a stone wall topped with a grille and lined with chicken wire, an instance of the islanders' thorough approach to partitioning and fencing.

One side of the schoolyard was assigned to boys, the other to girls. Though there was an unfenced passageway between the two, boys and girls never mingled; they could call to each other across the grille, but this never happened. They did not play together—it was not done. In Saint-Denis, relations between the sexes followed certain patterns that had puzzled us at first. We gathered that they all but precluded contacts between boys and girls outside of immediate family relationships. As a result, a secret electricity hung around the fence dividing the schoolyard in two.

At the back of the school were two small apartments. Monsieur Dupeux, the portly, jovial secretary of the Mairie, lived in one, and the director of the school and his wife, Monsieur and Madame Guyonnet, in the other. Monsieur Guyonnet, nicknamed Guilloupette by his students, had a leonine head atop a slightly built body. He wore golden pince-nez and a black suit and a tie at all times. My grandmother had called on him once and reported that he was a socialist of the old school, a very nice man—she had said that he looked like a kindly lion. We were skeptical: Guilloupette's manner in school was extremely forbidding.

The school and the Mairie had a special smell, a mixture of violet ink, the kind that is made in a big bottle from a powder of chalk mixed with Chlorox. To me, this was the smell of *laïcité*, that of the Ecole Communale, *laïque et obligatoire*. *Laïque* meant freedom from interference by the church. Although Maréchal Pétain wanted to do away with *laïcité*, it asserted itself through that smell. It was a declaration of independence not only from religion, but from the new government of France as well. From what we knew of Monsieur Guyonnet, we were confident that he would not let himself be intimidated by directives from Vichy. In school he never said a word in praise of the Maréchal, although he had had to hang a color photograph of the hero of Verdun in full marshal's uniform high above his desk.

Across the Place de la Mairie—but it really should have been Place de l'Eglise as a matter of historic precedence—the Romanesque church of Saint-Denis honoring an early Christian bishop testified to the antiquity of our village: Saint-Denis was the martyr who, after his own beheading, was said to have walked from Montmartre, Mont des Martyrs, to what became Saint-Denis near Paris, carrying his own head in his hands. Our church had been built under Eleanor of Aquitaine. Its harmonious façade was of pale gold limestone, carved with a simple crisscross design. I often wondered who Saint-Denis really was. We now depended on his benevolence: he was our protector-saint.

Inside, the church was dank, filled with the odor of clericalism, very different from the smell of *laïcité*. It was a mixture of fading white lilies, fleshy and sweet, of incense and mold. André and I were distressed by the smell of the school—it was sterile, suggesting order and responsibility. But the sickly sweet smell of the church where we were taken once in a while on Sundays by Natasha distressed us even more. Yet secretly, each time I set forth for church, I experienced a sense of anticipation. Unlike André, who was irritated by my fondness for clothes, I enjoyed dressing up. I liked to look at the Bourrade girls in their new powder blue Sunday coats—the Bourrades were devoted churchgoers. Moreover, nothing would have pleased me more than being touched by God's Grace and believing in Him. He would have helped settle a number of questions I was finding troublesome. I fervently hoped that I might have a religious experience as we sat through the endless midday Mass in the cold church. What if God were to speak to me? But nothing at all happened under the gray arches bathed in dim, greenish light. The smell of decaying flowers was overpowering. The service conducted in a French-accented Latin was tedious, and the singing was thin, like an acid wine. Every minute in church dragged on like an hour.

André and I eventually decided that we would not go to church any more. How we wished we also could say *no* to school! Having tasted of country roaming and wild beaches, Paul, André, and I now felt like adults. For a time, while Maréchal Pétain's "New Order" was establishing itself, classes were postponed from week to week in all of France. We had lived in the hope that school might never open again. But one morning, at the end of our endless summer, the three of us got up very early. We walked to school. We were losing our freedom once again. Only the *vendanges* gave us a little respite. Once in a while we were allowed to skip school for a half-day of grape cutting.

In the Ecole Communale of Saint-Denis, everything was done in a disciplinary fashion. Learning was achieved through memorizing summaries of subjects that were strictly determined by a governmental program. Things were easier for me than for André: the peasant boys were rougher than the girls. By disposition I was interested in pleasing. I was determined to excel in school. I felt that, as a foreigner and therefore an outcast, I had no other means of holding my own. I decided to be a good student and, at the same time, one of the girls who aroused interest among the boys on the other side of the fence. This was to be done by means of an imperceptible flirtatiousness. Above all, André was not to suspect anything. He despised what he called my "girlishness," and I valued his esteem. I pursued my double goal with determination, while unsuspecting adults praised me for my good manners and my exemplary behavior: *"Comme elle est sage!"* ("What a good girl!"). My attitude gave me impetus enough to hold my own with my new classmates.

Unlike the boys, the girls of Saint-Denis scared me. They were muscular and tough. They dressed like scaled-down adults in black *blouses* (housecoats of cotton sateen); in long woolen stockings held up by heavy metallic garters, and clanging sabots. They had only disdain for the stranded Parisians who had intruded on their world at the beginning of the war. The girls' behavior was tamer on the surface than the boys', but underneath there was a hidden hysteria as high-pitched as their voices, ready to burst forth. When they were excited, they quickly used foul language and ear-splitting shrieks. They made allusions to sex which I did not catch. They whispered to each other and hid their mouths when they laughed. Some were excellent students, while others were almost illiterate, but they all knew how to milk cows, to clean fish, and to kill chickens.

Among them I had felt conspicuous in my white blouse and pleated skirt—and under it, no slip or petticoat. A home-sewn petticoat of coarse linen cloth was part of the peasant girls' uniform and, I gathered, a symbol of modesty. But I had never owned anything resembling a petticoat. I only wore white knitted cotton pants under my navy skirt. From the start this had created a sensation in my class. I had the choice of persuading my mother to make me a petticoat at once, or to make do without one. I decided to do the latter, saying in an offhand way that I found petticoats a hindrance. After an excruciating period—for a while I saw myself as the young Spartan boy with a fox under his shirt—the girls of Saint-Denis began to ask their mothers to let them go to school without petticoats. Time went by, and two or three students in my class became my close friends, but that took forever to happen.

The Intruder

I have no distinct recollection of the departure from our island of our various summer visitors. But I do remember that even before the good weather was over the Germans had decreed that people who were not permanent residents of Oléron could not stay: our island was becoming a part of a restricted military zone. Having arrived the year before, we were regarded as local inhabitants, but Clara had to go to the Kommandantur to request permission to remain on the island. Colonel Schmidt had received her in private. She explained to him that we were her adoptive family, that she had no other relatives in France. On the spot, as she sat in his cozy office in the back of Villa Adrienne, the colonel signed an ordinance waiver for her and for Paul.

Clara reported that, as was said in the village, Colonel Schmidt was indeed "very correct." The colonel could not be a Nazi—there had been a spontaneous understanding between him and Clara. He had asked several questions about us, and Clara had answered them brilliantly. She had said that we were authentic White Russians living in France since the early twenties. When she had explained that my grandmother was a *grande dame* who had lost everything in the Revolution, that our family was fervently devoted to the monarchy, waiting from year to year for the Romanovs to return to Russia, he had been particularly sympathetic.

Jokingly, my father asked whether the time had not come to hang a portrait of the late Tzar Nicholas in the Ardeber dining room. Everyone laughed except my grandmother, who, as an old revolutionary, was offended, exclaiming, *"Jamais!"* But more than anyone she rejoiced that Clara and Paul would be staying on in Saint-Denis.

During these weeks in the late summer of 1940, when the Fedotovs left for America and when, to Clara's distress, even the Kalitas and the Martins and their entourage returned to Paris, my grandmother sometimes spoke longingly of the prospect of obtaining a visa for the United States. Her daydreaming was infectious; I used to try to imagine our arrival, aboard the glorious *Normandie,* in a new country where there would be no Germans and nothing to fear.

But soon my grandmother came to terms with our fate. Of all the inhabitants of the Maison Ardeber, she turned out to be the most imaginative in enhancing our day-to-day life. She learned how to make, with only a trace of sugar, a kind of grape jam, called *raisiné*. Remembering Russia during the Revolution, she and the young Chernushkis pioneered the picking and drying of mushrooms, which we found under the island's woods throughout the fall.

That fall, the older children sometimes went along to work

with one or the other *vendangeurs* in our family. To me, the lovely part of the *vendanges* was the ride in and out of Saint-Denis in a lumbering horsedrawn wooden cart, sitting very high atop the tall, oval wooden barrels in which the grapes were taken back to the village. From their swaying heights, the view of the countryside was startling—the old windmills dotting the horizon were like sentinels guarding the sea, a ribbon of silver severed only to the south in the direction of Méray, where the land widened. There, on a windy, clear day, one could see the towering elms near Julien's house.

The weather changed a week or ten days before the *vendanges* ended. A cold rain fell. In the vineyards the earth turned to mud, and the grapes started rotting. Every night, the *vendangeurs* returned in the dark, soaked throughout, sticky with grape juice that had an overpowering sweet-and-sour smell. The *vendanges* became a torture for the Chernushkis, but my father never minded them. By then he was already walking around Saint-Denis in clanging, straw-filled sabots.

The *vendangeurs* would wash in turn in our kitchen, then they would set their wet clothing to dry before the stove. Eventually, all of us would sit down to a supper which grew less abundant with each day. The *vendanges,* with their promised allocation of potatoes and grain, were our main hope for survival. They alone enabled us to subsist through that winter on Oléron.

I remember a dinner at the Maison Ardeber toward the end of the *vendanges*. Despite the pine cones flaming in the enameled stove in the dining room, it was cold. Wet clothes were spread out around it to dry. The meal was thin oatmeal soup flavored with mushrooms. I remember looking at my mother across the table: she was so pale that I felt a pang of anxiety. Since childhood, she had been the most delicate of the three Chernushkis.

Next to her at the table, Clara looked rested and soignée: she had spent the day writing letters to would-be employers on the island. She was wearing that tight-fitting woolen jumpsuit that she had inherited from her tour of duty in the Spanish civil war.

Sitting by his mother, Paul was frowning at his porridge. I was sympathetic. I, too, detested oatmeal. But when Paul deliberately spilled the sticky whitish liquid, I was disgusted. Better to eat the soup than look at it, spreading slowly over the ancient, cracked oilcloth. When Clara jumped up from the table, I assumed that she might be on her way to the kitchen to find a sponge, but instead she seized Paul in her arms and pressed him against her, covering him with kisses. Then she called, "My little Paul! *Mon pauvre petit! Mon fiston!*" She turned to my father and cried out, "How can you sit here and do nothing? We soon will all die of hunger! My poor child, *mon fiston*! Don't just sit here! Do something!"

My father remained calm—but there was a threatening note in his voice as he said, after a pause, in an extremely polite manner, "Clara, why don't you join in the *vendanges* like everyone else? *Comme tout le monde?* As I see it, this is the only way to increase our food reserves for the winter." Clara, still hugging Paul, turned red. She said, "I am not *tout le monde!*" and left the room.

While Ariadne was cleaning the table with a damp rag, and my mother went off to fetch Clara and try to explain that my father had not meant to hurt her feelings, my grandmother rushed to the kitchen. She returned holding up three eggs which the Michaux, for whom my father worked, had given to him that evening. *Pour les petits,* meaning for the three little boys. Then she was back in the kitchen, making an omelette for Clara and Paul. It was all very strange—I felt that the Maison Ardeber was becoming bewitched.

By 1941, regardless of the seasons, our days on Oléron were like the small rounded stones on the beach, innumerable, interchangeable. Yet, if one looks closely at one of the pebbles that cover the expanse of Grande Plage at low tide, it has its own way of being rounded and gray and smooth. So had our days on Oléron. The succession of those identical days felt like eternity. When I sometimes rage at how swiftly time flows now, I realize that, on Oléron, I tasted of eternity. One cannot expect, nor want, this to happen more than once in a lifetime.

Unlike the years that followed, 1940 had been eventful from beginning to end. Some days had been dazzling, others had been heavy as boulders, and one was like an explosion—the afternoon I discovered how I felt about Clara. That fall afternoon is the most vivid of my wartime memories. Nothing was the same after that. Even my infatuation with Julien became less absorbing.

Later, thinking back to that time, I kept wondering why this recognition was linked in my memory with the chestnut tree in the garden of the Maison Ardeber. And then one day not too long ago, I remembered. It had happened like this: I was looking for horse chestnuts under our tree, planning to make a necklace out of the smooth brown nuggets that shone so appealingly through the cracks of the prickly green skins.

As I leaned to pick one up, I realized that each of these bright green balls had been in springtime, in what seemed another life—before the Germans had come to Oléron—a bright pink blossom. These had been in bloom while we were all helping my grandmother and Clara move into the salon. I remembered how I had studied them, opening and closing the doors of the *armoire à glace,* watching the patterns made on the walls by the reflected green leaves and pink flowers. With the recollection of that slightly hypnotic movement of flowers and leaves came a surge of feeling like a physical spasm. When it subsided, I discovered that what was possessing me was hatred for Clara Rittoni.

That beautiful blond woman was not at all what she had seemed in those spring days—she was not white and pure. Why was she among us? By what right? She was an intruder. I wanted her to vanish. I would never have another moment of peace until she left our house. From the beginning, she had been taking advantage of the Chernushkis. She was using my grandmother in a hundred different ways. She was evil. I suddenly remembered the swollen, arthritic Ida Samoylovna. She, too, had used my grandmother, and evil had come of it. Clara had to leave at once.

I felt an extraordinary sense of freedom. It was as if everything inside me was clarified. Not that the world was losing its threatening quality—the German soldiers with their inquisitive, jovial faces were still walking up and down rue du Port. In the depths of our house, day and night, we could hear their boots on the pavement. There were many battles to be fought, yet within our family order would be reestablished as soon as Clara left.

I dropped my handful of horse chestnuts to the ground and climbed onto the "thinking wall." My grandmother's adoration of Clara must have been contagious—why else would I have been so slow to understand her? Clara did not love us. She considered us stupid and dowdy, yet she had to have the shelter of our roof. When had she done anything for any member of our family? To present us as pro-German to Colonel Schmidt—for that, in effect, was what she had done the other day—was self-serving, as well as dishonorable.

Clara despised the young Chernushkis for their gentleness and their desire to help others. I could not remember ever hearing her utter a word of thanks for anything that was done for her, nor for the presents my grandmother had been showering on her and Paul since their arrival in Saint-Denis. Only the other day, Clara had tried to appropriate my mother's beautiful black satin suit, saying lightly, "You'll let me have it, won't you, Olga? It is a little too big for you. You can't say no. . . ."—and my mother had *not* said no, without having quite said yes. Only when my grandmother had remarked that the suit should naturally belong to the one real blond in the family had she said no sharply.

I could almost hear the drone of Clara's voice demanding that "something be done to improve our diet"—yet she never went shopping for provisions in the village. She did not cook; she never entered the kitchen, except to fetch hot water for her or Paul's bath. I had never seen her wash a dish—cold water hurt her delicate skin. When dishwashing time came and the Chernushkis carried dishes back into the kitchen, heating up a bucket of water and heroically scouring pots with a little sand—soap and powders had disappeared from our lives—Clara would get up too, and pace the room, stopping once in a while to warm her hands before the stove. While doing this, she would discourse in a loud voice.

Clara described in detail how only the year before in Paris, a famous Italian anarchist had committed suicide for love of her.

Often, she gave practical advice. As the Chernushkis moved from dining room to kitchen and back, they would listen with distracted equanimity. Clara had the best information about how to wash clothes with wood ashes; about luscious desserts that could be made without milk and eggs: "Before she left for Paris, Madame Kalita told me that there are certain seaweeds to be found right here on Oléron. Besides containing gelatin, they actually taste like fresh strawberries. Shouldn't Vadim look into the matter?"

Only once had one of the Chernushkis talked back to Clara. That was when she had proposed that the women in our family, like all the other women on the island, raise rabbits in the Ardeber garden. Within six months these would provide all the protein the children needed in their diet. She said, her voice becoming more and more insistent, "We will have to have about four dozen rabbits. Madame Braud has promised to give us three pregnant mother-rabbits. Let Vadim build some cages. The best way to build cages is the following . . ."

Suddenly Aunt Ariadne said in an unnaturally clear voice, "Why not, dear Clara? At once! Let us start an *élevage de lapins*! But, since we are busy with the small children and with other chores, and Mother does much of the cooking, we will do it on one condition—you will be the one to clean the rabbit cages. . . ."

Turning bright red, Clara had exclaimed, "I, clean rabbit cages? You can't be serious, Ariadne!" The subject of the *élevage de lapins* was dropped.

I kept remembering the hundred small things that made me hate Clara. I felt petty, yet I could not stop: one memory led to another; they were magnified in my mind like brief, theatrical scenes. As I sat on the "thinking wall" just above the spot where, according to Clara's plans, the rabbits were to live, my loathing for her welled up again. Now it was filling my whole being. On whom but Clara could I blame this dreadful feeling? For this, I hated her even more. Then I had another thought, and now I hated myself—I knew that secretly I myself once had wanted to be like Clara.

I tried to share my insights into Clara with other members of the family, but to my astonishment, I had little success in opening their eyes to Clara's true nature. But I do not remember ever trying to discuss her with my grandmother—it would have been useless. My grandmother did not believe that anyone around her could be evil. Only distant, semimythical figures like Stalin or Attila could be evil. I knew even then that she was one of the world's innocent troublemakers who give their love to countless persons and expect to be loved back by each of them. This complete confidence was what had made her a miracle-maker— and also now a disaster-maker.

    I did speak to my parents about Clara one afternoon. We went for a walk along the jetty, in my favorite "father-daughter-mother" formation—I between my parents, holding each by the hand. After hearing me out, my father told me that I was greatly exaggerating Clara's villainy, but that, in fact, he himself was not fond of her. But he wanted me to understand that as the man in our household, he could not in time of danger be unchivalrous to a woman alone with a child. Intuitively, I had known for a long time that my father did not care for Clara, yet at that moment to hear him tell me this was the most important thing in the world.

    I then asked my mother *why* she was always so patient with Clara. In a trembling voice, she said that, on the contrary, she had always held her own with Clara, that she had rebutted her when she had criticized me in private for my "lack of team spirit." Perhaps Clara resented the fact that I was a better student than Paul? My mother was upset. I had to understand that neither she nor her sisters would turn the Maison Ardeber into a battlefield for warring mothers. This would be against the traditions of our family. Clara would soon be moving out—she was making arrangements with Mademoiselle Charles to rent rooms in the back of her house. These would be quite separate, opening as they did on a small back lane linking rue du Port to the center of the village.

After this conversation, which had left me only partly appeased—my parents had refused to see how treacherous Clara was—I decided not to mention my insights to my aunts. My mother's reaction, when I had mentioned her lack of assertiveness, had been a warning signal. All I could do now was to watch Clara guardedly. I was powerless against her presence in our midst.

Clara did move into Mademoiselle Charles's house soon afterward, just as my mother had said, but this made little difference: she and Paul continued to take their meals with us. As winter came and we spent more time indoors, the occasions multiplied when, warming herself at our enameled stove, Clara imparted her thoughts and her advice to our family. I would shut myself up in my parents' bedroom upstairs, but even there I could hear her foretelling our future. I knew what she was saying: the war was lost, it was only a matter of weeks before a German landing expedition would sweep into England and conquer it.

I knew that my family had an almost mystical belief that Hitler could not win the war, that he was too corrupt. This belief kept the adults going, yet with Clara they failed to make a case for it. Her arguments, gleaned from her new acquaintances within the bourgeoisie of Saint-Denis, rested on complex, ever-shifting strategical considerations. When someone finally raised an objection in a soft voice, Clara would toss her blond hair back with an elegant gesture and say contemptuously, "Of course, you can't understand. You are so old-fashioned! You are out of touch with things—idealists always are."

Lying on my parents' bed, trying to read, I could hear my grandmother punctuate Clara's words with a soft, even *"oui, oui, oui."* Where was my grandmother who could bring so much fire to an argument when it captured her imagination? Sometimes I thought that Clara had cast a spell on everyone around me. At other moments, I feared that she was a sign of things to come—of what people would be after Hitler's victory. This thought filled me with a sorrow I can still taste today.

No tremor rocked the Maison Ardeber when Clara went to work for the Germans. Was it because the adults now were beginning to be frightened of her? The news came with a flourish one evening in January: Colonel Schmidt had offered her a job at the Kommandantur.

We were at supper at the Maison Ardeber. *Un silence gêné* ("a troubled silence") greeted Clara's words. I remember thinking: How predictable it all is! How revolting! Now Clara is going to work for the Germans to help them win the war, and all we will do is remain silent. Instead of an outcry, a great scandal, all there is here is embarrassment—a troubled silence, a troubled silence—and I kept repeating to myself these words like an incantation, still hoping that my father would forget his sense of chivalry (or was it concern for our safety?) and break the spell by throwing Clara out of our house.

But there was only a silence that lasted and lasted. What

was, in effect, a clear demonstration of Clara's unworthiness was resulting not in her flight from our house, but in her entrenchment among us. My grandmother still believed in her goodness. Already she was repeating her soft-voiced *"oui, oui, oui,"* as Clara enumerated the advantages of her serving as a benevolent intermediary between the Occupation armies and the French population. Her friend was sacrificing herself for our sake and the people of Saint-Denis. As for my parents and my two aunts, they seemed too stunned to say anything. Now Clara had a direct connection with the Germans—and she knew all about our family's anti-Fascist convictions.

Clara was savoring her new power. Her audience's lack of response only made her stretch out her tale. Unable to find a job on the island and without consulting anyone, because from her childhood she had relied on herself alone in crucial moments, she had gone to Colonel Schmidt to request a safe conduct for Toulouse, where the Modiglianis were awaiting her. Once again, the colonel had led her into his private office in the back of Villa Adrienne. He had been willing to give her an exceptional document permitting her to go to Toulouse; Clara and Paul were privileged because of their Austro-Italian background.

At his desk, leaning back in his chair, the colonel had suddenly put down his fountain pen. "My dear Madame Rittoni," he had said in a solemn voice. "You have a mission right here! Why don't you become our interpreter? The young lady who has been working for us is a Jewess. She was a good worker, but the time has come for her to go. All Jews must leave the island. We need someone trustworthy, a person whom the civilian population would respect. With your splendid education, your knowledge of both German and French, not to mention your Italian, your charm. . . . Why, you are ideal for this well-remunerated post. Your White Russian friends will be overjoyed to have you stay on."

How could Clara refuse? It might have been dangerous: one did not say *no* to the Germans. It was our happy star that had inspired Colonel Schmidt to make this proposal. Now she would be able to pay her own and Paul's share of household expenses and help us survive in Saint-Denis. "Through the Germans I will also be able to obtain certain provisions," Clara said. "Colonel Schmidt has hinted that while I work for them I will enjoy certain privileges."

Clara continued to take her meals with us, using our dining room night after night as a stage. However, German foodstuffs never materialized on our table—my father had told her that no German donation was ever to appear at the Maison Ardeber.

The only German food that we were ever to eat was some round loaves of black bread thrown to us over the "thinking wall" by a half-crazed Pole. The man was taking care of horses in a requisitioned stable at the back of the second garden. But this was later: the Pole, who spoke incoherently to himself, had been driven mad by something he had experienced on the Russian front. He spoke Polish, a language we almost, but not quite, understood. The loaves of bread he threw over the wall spoke for themselves, like words of kindness.

Social Life Under the Nazis

One day the Alsatian refugees were taken away from Saint-Denis on "orders from above," for the local German authorities did not particularly mind their presence in the village. We had no notion of it then, but among those departing were twelve-year-old André Schwartz-Bart and his family, all eventually taken to an extermination camp. Young André escaped and joined the underground. Later he wrote *The Last of the Just.*

In the company of my Aunt Natasha and my cousin André, I went to say good-bye to an Alsatian boy called David whom André had befriended at school. I remember a row of open trucks parked in front of the church, their engines idling. The Alsatians' departure was, like their arrival in Saint-Denis, bewildering, because of their dark winter clothing, and the sadness in their eyes. They, who had blended with the people of Oléron in the summer, again looked alien, weighed down by some yet unnamed curse. Although this departure took place at high noon, there is a twilight coloration to my recollection of it.

Clara's theatrics, giving us daily reports on the lives and thoughts of the German officers in Saint-Denis, were also night scenes. Her stories were about German officers who had fallen in love with her. Firmly she repulsed their advances, yet romantic friendships blossomed because of the officers' infinite respect for her. Daringly, Clara would then reveal her own critical feelings about Hitler. Her admirers, overcome by her bravery, in turn put their lives into her hands. They, too, felt that the Führer was vulgar, that he was given to excesses.

One evening Clara told us about a highly significant encounter she had had with Colonel Schmidt. That day he had asked her to attend to some routine problem of stable requisitioning. As she was leaving, the colonel had called her back in a most polite manner: "By the way, dear Madame Rittoni, do you know a Frau von Wittenghof-Kalita? We have just received a letter from her. It appears that this lady has three sons by her first marriage to a member of the Baltic nobility. These three brave, able-bodied young men are now fighting under the German flag. She and her second husband, a White Russian by the name of Herr Kalita, are requesting a permit to settle in Saint-Denis. It is a pity that we can't allow anyone to move into the military zone." The colonel picked up from his desk what was evidently Madame Kalita's letter. Sighing, he tore it in two and dropped it in his wastebasket.

Clara had resolutely walked to the colonel's desk. Standing erect, she had spoken in a clear, persuasive voice, which she now endeavored to reproduce: "Yes, Colonel Schmidt, I know the Kalitas," she had said. "They are highly estimable people. For the good of your own country, you should not treat such people in this insensitive fashion. Why don't you authorize the brave mother of three German warriors to reside on the island? The

Kalitas could serve as a bridge between the French and the Occupation armies. Madame Kalita, a lady of refinement, would become a civilizing force and help achieve an honorable collaboration."

Clara bent down and plucked the two halves of Madame Kalita's letter out of the wastebasket. She put them before the colonel, pushing the torn parts together on his desk. He was so moved by her boldness and her generosity of spirit that he had her sit down at a typewriter immediately. He dictated a letter to Herr and Frau Kalita in Paris, granting them the right to settle within the military zone, which was becoming known throughout Europe as the Atlantic wall.

The Kalitas arrived in Saint-Denis by bus, accompanied by their noisy white terrier, Bebka. The rickety bus, piloted by Monsieur Glodon, was almost totally filled with their luggage, including many magnificent presents for Paul and Clara. I recollect in particular that something indescribably sophisticated and costly, a perfume called "Amour, Amour" de Jean Patou, was presented to Clara—but I do not remember ever smelling it. Once again, the Kalitas settled near Place de l'Ormeau in that commodious cottage on the property of Madame Marquet, a member of the local bourgeoisie, which they had occupied the summer before.

At once Andrei Kalita started to garden. Fear of starvation, it appeared, had brought the Kalitas back to the island. *Elevages* were inaugurated on a big scale, in wire cages erected by André Kalita in the middle of Madame Marquet's well-kept, turn-of-the-century garden. Clara was enthusiastic; here were rabbits and ducks, and even geese. Madame Kalita toiled from dawn to dusk to feed them, gathering special herbs and periwinkles, and chopping these together to make a nutritious pâté.

In addition to the raising of vegetables, her husband devoted himself to a certain amount of commerce with the Occupation forces: he acted as a middleman between Germans and local peasants. People in the village criticized the Kalitas, although no one knew about Madame Kalita's sons in the German army. They were harsher on Clara Rittoni, a provocative single woman. She was known in the village as *"La Tarpette,"* for *l'interpète,* or *"l'Autrichienne,"* for Marie Antoinette: *"Elle se donne des airs,"* Madame Braud remarked to the Chernushkis: "Unlike you, she gives herself airs."

With his excellent German and his bon vivant tastes—he was a connoisseur of wines and something of a drinking man—Andrei Kalita turned out to be the perfect intermediary between the Germans and those peasants who were anxious to sell their wines to the Occupation forces at exorbitant prices. The jovial Kalita was skillful and discreet. His activity was profitable and also reassuring; it eradicated any likelihood of famine striking the Kalita household. Grateful customers presented them with fabulous foodstuffs. Chocolate, noodles, and cigarettes came from the Germans, while the French supplied lard and eggs. Once in a while, Kalita acted as an unofficial negotiator in everyday matters between Germans and French. His services left both sides satisfied.

Clara and Paul spent a great deal of time with their friends. To my indignation, which I had trouble hiding, my family was drawn into seeing them too. Vera Kalita would drop by the Maison Ardeber and my grandmother would ask her to stay for tea; Andrei Kalita sought my father's advice on gardening. Madame Kalita, the mother of three sons, adored young boys. She soon included André in her circle of favorites. To his despair, she decided that my cousin had to be fattened. I remember her bringing a cold cooked omelette to the Maison Ardeber especially for him. My fastidious cousin was mortified. I felt triumphant: no one cared if I was skinny or not. I was excluded from the Kalitas' benefactions. I was reading Lamartine's history of the French Revolution, lent to me by Julien: my heroes, Danton and Mirabeau, would not have been invited to tea at the Kalitas.

The Kalitas were not the only people in Saint-Denis to be fearful of hunger. The winter had been hard: the small boys had not grown at all, and the Chernushkis and my father had lost weight. In 1941 my father decided to put all his forces and his imagination into gardening. His greatest obstacle was the lack of land—he had found some tools in the chaotic accumulation of objects in the Ardeber barn across the street, and Mademoiselle Charles had given him permission to repair and use them. But fallow land was unavailable around Saint-Denis.

Finally, a neighbor agreed to let my father use a small field below us on rue du Port, with the provision that one-third of the crops would go to him. My father started clearing it in late February, and this took weeks. Mademoiselle Charles, more generous, put a parcel of overgrown dune at his disposal, without any precise conditions attached to it, although she did expect small favors, like moving a trunk or fixing her gate, in exchange for it. Potatoes were known to have grown there once. It was located in a beautiful isolated spot along Côte Sauvage and became my father's favorite field—he wrote a series of poems about it.

My father had never gardened before, but he loved the earth, he loved Oléron, and from the beginning his crops were spectacular. Besides the security of knowing that we would all have enough to eat year round, what I liked best about my father's gardening was the elegance he brought to it. How royally he walked up and down rue du Port, pushing before him the ancient Ardeber wheelbarrow, his sabots resounding proudly on the pavement. How shiny his tools were—the antique mattocks and the shovels, which he had lovingly fitted with new, hand-carved handles. And how gracefully and vigorously his rows of climbing green beans, corn, and tobacco plants grew and reached to the sky!

I myself could not stand dropping dry peas into small holes, or worse, weeding for hours on end. I helped at home instead. This enabled me to appreciate my father's gardening from an aesthetic point of view. His domain broadened from year to year: he had separate fields in various sections of Saint-Denis, doing extra work for the land's proprietors in place of paying rent.

The peasants of Saint-Denis, who had snickered at first when a Parisian had started to till the earth, now treated him as an equal. Since my father had no horses or plow, and tractors were unknown in Saint-Denis, he had to do everything by hand. This appealed to them, they liked things done the hard way: on Oléron there was competition as to who would be more frugal with more ostentation. But the peasants of Oléron were also pragmatists: my father's tomatoes became famous in the village—they ripened in early June. His fields, fertilized only with seaweed, were luxuriant.

Clara's dream of a cultured social life, bringing together the German officers and the elite of Saint-Denis, with herself as a presiding deity, came true for a while—until Russia, that "land of savages," as she was to call it, engulfed the distinguished graying officers and the vigorous young men who left for the plains of Russia, never to return. Before the tide turned and Germans all but disappeared from our island, to be replaced by urbane Austrians, stubby, frightened Czechs, flaxen-haired Poles, and black-eyed Italians, there was an interlude when collaboration flowered in Saint-Denis.

In an effort to win the sympathies of the civilian population the Germans organized children's parties at Christmastime. The notables of the village were invited for coffee at Villa Adrienne. German movies were shown on Sundays in the ballroom of the Hotel Gai Soleil. I remember a poster announcing the showing of *The Jew Süs,* displayed on the wall of the Mairie. I do not recall exactly how it looked, except that it was purple and yellow and so hideous that I could not bear to look at it. Filled with revulsion and fear, I kept thinking of our close friends in Paris from whom we had no news—the Lutzkys whom I loved, the Landesmans, the Zelenskys.

The crowning event of this period was the formal dinner Colonel Schmidt gave in honor of Clara and Madame Kalita. Clara talked about it for days—I remember every detail of it, as if I had been there, much better than any formal affair I have since attended in person.

The dinner was given in the ballroom of the Hotel Gai Soleil, which was decorated for the occasion with Nazi flags and red carnations. The German officers wore their dress uniforms. A military band, having performed the Nazi anthem, went on to play softly some Viennese waltzes. There were some non-Germans present in addition to the Kalitas and Clara Rittoni, but they were not known in Saint-Denis.

In order to decide who would sit to the right of Colonel Schmidt, Clara Rittoni and Vera Kalita had to choose between a white and a red rose. Clara, asked to make her selection first, naturally took the white one—and found herself to the right of the colonel. Madame Kalita with her red rose was placed to the right of Colonel Schmidt's adjutant. But the fact that her younger friend was the center of attention did not offend Madame Kalita, quite the opposite. Her feelings for Clara were passionate. Whenever she called on my grandmother, Vera Kalita could speak of nothing but Clara and Paul. While as friendly as ever, Clara now sometimes asserted her independence in unpredictable ways, and this worried Madame Kalita.

Delicious foods were served at that dinner—chicken breasts in cream sauce and ice cream, unheard of since the beginning of the war. Then champagne was poured out for the guests, who sat at long tables covered with white cloths. Colonel Schmidt proposed a toast to the Führer and then to the health of Madame Rittoni, Clara, "that pure, clear vision of womanhood who reminds us of our own wives and sweethearts at their noblest. . . ." Afterward the guests danced to waltzes played by the military band.

ISLAND IN TIME

There are happy memories out of that time also, yet they too are memories of twilight—particles of happiness suspended in the all-permeating anxiety that was our life. There were bicycle expeditions to look for mushrooms in the woods of Boyardville along the southeastern coast of the island, where dusk would steal upon us, the smells of seaweed and resin mingling in the wondrous smell of fall on Oléron. Suddenly, it would be too dark to see the mushrooms against their russet beds of pine needles. We hurried back toward our bicycles at the edge of the woods. Sometimes we lost our way, but this would be only slightly disturbing. I was never really frightened whenever my father was along, and we never went to far-away Boyardville without him. Madly we would bicycle back to Saint-Denis for fear that we would be late for the curfew. The baskets of mushrooms and bulging bags of prickly pine cones tied to our handlebars bounced against our knees, making our bikes unsteady.

Often Ariadne came along, and I'd team up with her. The most Russian of the three young Chernushkis, she was a creature of the woods. Even her nickname, Aooka, an invention of the Russian–Parisian writer Remizov, was derived from the sound Russians use to call to each other in the woods: "Aooo!" She was uncanny at finding mushrooms. As we walked in the forest she would recite poetry by heart for hours on end: these expeditions were free of the unhappiness that was now at the core of my life.

So were Julien's visits to the Maison Ardeber. I can see myself dressing up for a costume party organized by the Chernushkis one evening when he was to spend the night at our house. I am standing before Ariadne's mirror, a Ukrainian maiden in an old, wide-sleeved, embroidered Russian shirt of Natasha's. I am trying on Ariadne's green Venetian beads and her orchid-shaped silver ring, which long afterward she gave me. My hair is shoulder length; I am growing it in an effort to win Julien's attention. My mother is standing in the doorway, a marquise with her hair powdered, which is extremely becoming to her. Her bouffant skirt is made from blue toile de Jouy found in one of the Ardeber armoires. Ariadne and André are musketeers in large hats decorated with tissue-paper feathers, wearing black moustaches and goatees drawn with burnt cork.

Our literary evenings were the glorious events of that time—with my passions for Julien and for poetry coming together in one celebration. To my joy, Clara, who was not interested in literature, retired early on these occasions, despite my grandmother's insistence that she stay on and read to us out of her favorite Italian author, D'Annunzio. And whenever they took place, Julien spent the night at our house, settling in André's room, the one with the pickled snake inside the writing desk, which had become my cousin's own room since Paul had moved away.

To have Julien sleep at our house was the greatest conceivable delight: not only was poetry read after dinner as late as midnight, or even one o'clock, but we also visited at breakfast, eating bread with *raisiné*, and drinking coffee brewed with home-roasted barley. At such moments I was thankful to the Germans for instituting a curfew that made it impossible for Julien to bicycle home at night.

Despite the shortage of flour and sugar, my grandmother always managed to bake something for our *soirée littéraire*. It might be a *galette*, a dry, sweet pastry, or a *clafoutis*, a deep-dish pie. My grandmother was liked by everyone in Saint-Denis—by Madame Bouchat, who would give her, with a wink of complicity, a small paper bag filled with flour; and by the dour *epicière*, who suddenly produced for her, and her alone, a tiny package, fifty grams of butter, more than enough to make a galette.

I remember thinking of Madame Lutin as I waxed the table in the dining room in preparation for a literary evening. I tried to set the table as elegantly as possible. The decorations made by Natasha or my mother would be unexpected and lovely—bouquets of old Ardeber lace and beads, or a still life of pine cones. Then suddenly it was a party; the ladies looked beautiful in their best dresses, with mascara and polished fingernails. Everyone gathered around the dining room table, where my grandmother served tea and the sweets she had prepared.

Julien and my father would start the evening by reading their new poems. Natasha might have prepared a translation of a story by Remizov. Ariadne recited poems by Tsvetayeva, which my grandmother then rendered in French, improvising the translation as she went on. My mother worked on translations of Mandelstam's *Tristia* into French, and I sometimes helped her.

Julien's poems were elliptic, yet they did speak obliquely about Oléron and the war engulfing the whole world:

> Sleek medusa, dew of the sea,
> The sun makes you grow.
> The sun lingers on the stones,
> Like a golden frost, war seizes the world.

After the reading there always was a spirited discussion, *à la Russe*. Julien took an impish delight whenever arguments became heated; these were unheard of in his family. With playful perversity, he tried to fan them, and was astonished when they evaporated, being only literary disagreements.

War with Russia

When on June 22, 1941, Hitler sprang his attack on the USSR, throwing more than two hundred divisions into battle along a front two thousand kilometers long, many people around us were relieved. Natural order was reestablished, Hitler was again assuming his predestined role, that of destroyer of world communism. His victory over Stalin was inevitable—yet all over Europe, even in Germany, there were those who for the first time had hope. Germany might be defeated in Russia—not by Stalin, but by the country itself, by its land and its people, which had once stopped Napoleon.

Hitler came extraordinarily close to victory. Had he launched his Operation Barbarossa on May 1, as was first his intention, instead of late June, he might well have succeeded. His three-pronged offensive was aimed essentially at Leningrad and Moscow. The two Russian capitals, symbols of revolution, were to be razed. An armistice would be signed no later than January 1942.

I recall on that June day in Saint-Denis my family's mixture of grief and hope at hearing news of the offensive—the ignominious alliance between Germany and Russia had ended. The German soldiers raced along rue du Port, calling to each other. The French collaborators, led by the curé, gathered on Place de la Mairie, discussing the events delightedly in the midsummer twilight. But there were shadows on the faces of the German soldiers. Their hope that war would soon end was fading. These soldiers were unfamiliar to us: a complete turnover had taken place on Oléron in preparation for the invasion of Russia. We also had a new commandant in Saint-Denis: Colonel Schultz, who, though younger, was, according to Clara, no less mature and sensitive than Colonel Schmidt.

I can still see Clara walking into the Maison Ardeber on that June day. "It will all be over in less than a month! Colonel Schultz says so! They are taking prisoners by the tens of thousands!" Clara was exhilarated and did not hide it: my father was away in his fields at that hour.

Three or four days later my father was arrested by the French police, "for verification of identity." All men of Russian origin were taken to Royan on the mainland, to be checked out for possible connections with the USSR; yet Andrei Kalita was not arrested. My father was led away by two French policemen in uniform; he did not come back for four days. His arrest came as a blow: I have forgotten everything about it, except for the instant when he was taken away on foot in the bright sunlight along rue du Port. I do recall spending hours afterward sitting on the "thinking wall," waiting for him to return. There were soldiers taking care of horses on the other side of the wall, but the tall laurel bushes hid me completely. The German grooms were uncommunicative, elderly men, busy with their animals.

The following months were marked by German victories so huge it seemed that, indeed, Hitler was about to be victorious. Kiev, the mother of Russian cities, had fallen. My family was beginning to despair. Fresh details of German triumphs were related to us by a jubilant Clara: her hatred of Russia seemed to grow every day. The reports of German cruelties there did not upset her. These became known quickly; evidently the Germans had no instructions about hushing them. Slavs were an inferior race, to be destroyed or enslaved.

Germans who had served on the Russian front in the early battles began arriving on our island for periods of rest. Clara recounted to us the officers' tales, full of graphic touches about the dirty, illiterate Russian peasants covered with lice, living in squalor in wooden cabins. Yet she was careful not to speak about these things within my father's hearing. She feared that he might suddenly throw her out of the Maison Ardeber, and she still needed our family to give her respectability in Saint-Denis.

Finally, as winter neared, she and Paul stopped coming to our house for dinner. The supplies Clara obtained through the Germans made this unnecessary. The Rittonis did continue to have lunch with us. It was convenient for Clara, "a brave working mother," as Paul called her, to have a hot meal in the middle of the day. That is what I recall of that summer: at lunch time, a feeling of emptiness induced by Clara's recitation of gigantic Russian defeats; in the afternoon, Madame Kalita stopping for tea with my grandmother on her way back from gathering periwinkles for her ducks.

One afternoon my grandmother and I were alone at the

Maison Ardeber. André, if he was at home, was hiding in the remotest recesses of the house—he now considered Vera Kalita his personal torturer. Sipping fragrant linden tea, Madame Kalita asked my grandmother whether we had made plans for the coming winter. My father's garden would not be enough. She and Clara were worried; they sympathized with our family's principles, but the adults had a responsibility to the children. There was nothing unpatriotic about going to work as a domestic for the Germans, was there? For a few hours a day? Nounou, Madame Marquet's trusted old nurse, worked every day at the German officers' mess. In addition to a generous salary, she brought home a container of soup and even some meat on occasion.

My blood boiled as I heard this, but all my grandmother said in response to Madame Kalita was a distracted *"oui, oui, oui."* She then asked Madame Kalita about the art of roasting barley for coffee, which the Kalitas were reported by Clara to have mastered to perfection. Now Vera Kalita was looking in my direction. Evidently she thought that if I were not around, she might be able to be more outspoken with my grandmother.

My grandmother, unmindful of the fact that, in Vera Kalita's eyes, I was an intruder, soon went off to the kitchen to make fresh linden tea, leaving me alone with our guest. Madame Kalita and I glowered at each other. I remember a wild temptation to ask: "Dear Madame Kalita, how are your three sons? Are they fighting on the Russian front yet? How do they like it?"—but for the sake of my grandmother I said nothing. I had been asked by her never to mention her sons to Madame Kalita.

The colossal offensive ordered by Hitler in mid-November—800,000 men, 4,500 tanks—was miraculously stopped short of Moscow. Russian civilians, building a gigantic network of earthworks, saved the capital. They were helped by an early cold wave. Like Napoleon's soldiers, the Germans started to die of cold by the thousands. They had gone off to Russia without winter clothes.

Gloom descended upon the Germans, even those on remote Oléron. In school, on orders from the Pétain government, we were made to collect warm clothing. A student in my class was busy knitting mittens for the "heroic fighters against communism." Monsieur Guyonnet, director of the school, did not encourage such pastimes: "We are here to study," he told her sharply. Monsieur Guyonnet was fearless.

On December 7, after Pearl Harbor, Germany declared war on the United States. For us in Europe, it was the first promising development in years of disasters. It was the best Christmas present we could have.

Now that Clara was no longer giving them directives in her loud monotone, the Chernushkis started raising rabbits in the back of our garden. The difficulty with raising rabbits was not evident at first, but soon the small boys were falling in love with certain favorite ones. It was heartbreaking whenever one grew big enough to be eaten. The poor animal was spirited away at night to old Madame Braud across the street, who, for a small fee, killed it and readied it for cooking. Whenever I met Madame Braud in the street, she would ask—would it be she or we who would go to hell as punishment for the rabbit's death? I answered that she had nothing to fear, that *we* were the ones that were certain to go to hell. Despite her teasing and the bushy white moustache over her upper lip, Madame Braud was one of the friendlier old women in Saint-Denis.

In the beginning of 1942, just as the Germans were being stopped before Moscow, Andrei Kalita asked my father to lend him a hand in plowing a field. He offered to pay him in cash, and my father accepted. We needed money urgently. What Daniel was sending us was enough for only our basic necessities.

Andrei Kalita's project was to take five or six days, and he himself, a man bursting with physical energy, was to work together with my father. Digging the earth alongside him, my father made a discovery: under Kalita's gross exterior there was a Russian patriot, undone at the thought of Russia's suffering. With tears in his eyes, Kalita told about the atrocities that the Germans were perpetrating. He spoke about the hangings and the pillage, recounted with such candor by Germans returning from the Eastern front to rest on Oléron. German officers and petty officers were Kalita's drinking companions.

As long as Germans and Russians had had an alliance, Kalita had made the best of the opportunities on Oléron: food and drink were of the greatest importance to him. As he put it in French: *"Je dois bouffer, moi!"* Now he would have preferred to stop trading with the Germans, but this would have made him look suspicious. Instead he was turning to my father to help him make contacts with the French Resistance. There were rumors of underground activity on the island; the Germans were alarmed by acts of sabotage that were beginning to multiply throughout France.

My father was reticent at first, especially when the Resistance was mentioned. However, little by little, he became convinced of the other's sincerity. As they were reaching the end of their task and the field was readied for sowing, he told Kalita the disheartening truth—that despite his efforts at discovering it, he knew of no anti-German resistance operating in our region.

The apparition of a new, pro-Russian Andrei Kalita transformed our life. The Kalitas had brought a big AM-FM radio from Paris. It received Radio London and even Radio Moscow with clarity, in spite of the Germans' efforts at jamming these stations. The Kalitas kept their receiver hidden behind a row of books in the back bedroom of their cottage, in the depths of the walled-in Marquet garden. We went there regularly to hear the evening news. Madame Kalita listened avidly, terrified for the sake of her sons—two of whom were now fighting on the Russian front. Clara never came with us and, despite her closeness to the Kalitas, she knew nothing of Andrei's anti-German feelings.

The adults often took André and myself along. We were reliable, we never said anything to anyone for or against the Germans. Things were more difficult with the small boys. It was not possible to tell them that the smiling soldiers who tried to give them candy and asked them to pose for snapshots on the beach were "bad men." On the other hand, if these were not "bad men," why did the Chernushkis avoid them with such determination? For a long time the boys had played war games. They were Germans conquering Saint-Denis. They sang "Halli Hallo" and uttered ferocious cries picked up from the soldiers' daily drill on Place de la Mairie: *"Verboten! Achtung!"* Embarrassed before our neighbors, my grandmother tried to restrain them, but without success.

My brother Sasha realized first that the Germans were to be avoided, but without overt hostility. Kiska was a year younger, while my brother's contemporary, Aliosha, was by nature extremely outgoing, his Slavic face and his blond hair so very Aryan-looking that he captured on the spot the heart of every German in sight. Sasha, no less fair than Aliosha, had fiery dark brown eyes and a less trusting disposition.

In 1942, behind bolted shutters and doors, we sat in a narrow circle around the Kalitas' radio, straining to catch both the Allies' voices and the sound of German boots beyond the garden gate. On certain evenings, German soldiers called on Kalita to place wine orders with him. We remained hidden in the back room while he parlayed with them, getting rid of them as quickly as possible.

It was with the Kalitas that we followed the horrifying events of 1942. France was unified under an ever-tightening German military rule. Helped by certain Frenchmen, the police were intensifying the arrests of Jews and their mass deportations. Maréchal Pétain's ability to temporize had all but disappeared. On the island, the Germans became a little more morose with each week.

I remember how we listened to the news of the execution, in the town of Châteaubriant in the nearby Vendée, of twenty-seven hostages in retaliation for the murder of two German officers. The family of our neighbor Colonel Merle lived in Châteaubriant—the colonel himself had stayed on in Saint-Denis only in order to keep the Germans from requisitioning the family house.

The grumpy colonel with the look of a bulldog had become a friend. He loved my father, with whom he traded gardening secrets. When the Châteaubriant executions took place, all restraint between us was gone. Dropping by at the Maison Ardeber in the morning, something which was not normally done, the colonel let his anger against the Germans flow freely and loudly while the Chernushkis tried to comfort him with freshly brewed barley coffee and a *tartine*—a slice of bread spread with sugarless jam.

Colonel Merle was outraged by the execution of uninvolved civilian hostages even though they might be communists.

He stamped his feet as he paced our dining room. He swore that the time to act had come. The colonel declared that he would be on the lookout for Gaullist contacts among the retired French officers on the island, and he promised to share his findings with my father. Not all French officers were like Colonel Bourrade, whom Merle held in open contempt for his pro-German views.

In the beginning of 1942, the bulk of the German forces had survived in Russia by practicing what was known as the "hedgehog technique." Surrounded military units dug into the snow and fought back in one spot. Now their objective for the summer was becoming clear. It was the conquest, at any price, of Stalingrad.

In Hitler's mind, Stalingrad, the centrally located industrial city on the Volga, would be a pivotal point for a huge maneuver, the success of which was to make him a general equal to Alexander the Great. The fall of Stalingrad would strangle Russia. German armies were to converge on Stalin's city; there they were to divide and move on to conquer the world. One would join with Rommel's armies in Libya by way of Turkey and Syria; the other would meet with the Japanese forces in India, having first overtaken Iran.

The Russians knew that the battle for Stalingrad was decisive. On the Kalitas' radio we heard Stalin's desperate appeal: "The fate of the Russian people depends on this battle. Not a step back! We must fight as the soldiers of Alexander Nevsky and those of Kutuzov once did. We must be ready to die." The confrontation lasted five months. It was one of the most fearsome battles in history. By November, von Paulus's Sixth Army was encircled in a frozen, phantasmagoric city reduced to rubble. On February 2, 1943, the Germans capitulated: the Russians had taken 91,000 prisoners, including twenty-three generals and one marshal, von Paulus himself. Two hundred and forty thousand Germans had been killed. The Russian losses had been no less huge, but the battle was won. On our distant island we felt that it was on the banks of the two mythical Russian rivers with the folkloric nicknames, Mother Volga and Father Don, that the tide of World War II had turned.

During the battle of Stalingrad we went to the Kalitas every night to listen to Radio Moscow. Crouched around the big radio in its fancy veneer cabinet, we stayed in the back bedroom long past the curfew hour. Making our way home in the dark, we walked in complete silence along the lane that ran past Clara's window. A faint ray of light could be seen at the bottom of her tightly closed wooden shutters.

The lane was enclosed on both sides by high garden walls.

It curved slightly, opening onto rue du Port just above our house. We listened for patrols. If they were coming in our direction, we froze against the walls, hiding in the black shadows of the laurel bushes, which sent their thick, billowing foliage over the stucco walls. When the night was moonless, we reached for the walls and followed their invisible lead toward rue du Port, where we had to dash for the Ardeber garden. Today when I think of wartime Oléron, I can still feel the soft touch of the walls' plaster on my fingertips.

On the night of my thirteenth birthday, January 22, 1943, we were returning from the Kalitas. It was a very cold moonlit night. I was thinking of the Russians who had saved Russia at Stalingrad, those compatriots of mine whose faces and voices I could not begin to imagine. I did not even know how their uniforms looked—were they khaki, or green, or brown? Then another, visceral feeling came over me. I was no longer thinking about the men dying on the Volga, but about myself. Perhaps it was true, and we did have a future? I understood that never until that night had I shared my family's belief that the Germans were going to be defeated. What stretched before me in the velvety darkness of the curving lane was life, a lifetime—my future. Even the edging of light under Clara's shutters, which we were then passing on tiptoe, had lost its threatening glimmer.

Survival on Oléron

I was sitting on the highest step at the end of our jetty. From there one could see the azure outlines of La Rochelle, now often bombarded by the Allies in the middle of the night because it harbored a huge German submarine base. I was looking at the sea, golden under a golden sun, trying to recapture my impressions as I had walked down the jetty for the first time on the day of our arrival in Saint-Denis. Now I knew every rock and every sand dune along its three beaches. They were mine. The sea, once like a moving wall behind which we were prisoners, was in fact the element that one day would bring about our release.

With each day, the Germans seemed more frightened by the ocean. By 1943 they no longer played volley ball on the dunes. They did not go swimming. They had lost the ebullience of their first summers on the island. Methodically, they were building concrete fortifications all along the coastline. Our beaches were beginning to look like settings for some gigantic, mysterious battle about to unfold.

The Germans were no longer quartered in Saint-Denis, although they continued to claim the buildings requisitioned over the years, which stood abandoned, emptied of their contents, their doors and windows open to the winds. Nowadays they were securely encamped inside their batteries along the shore, with their antiaircraft installations, with heavy cannons and nests of machine guns hidden under camouflage netting. Electrified barbed wire and mine fields surrounded them.

Day and night, trucks drove past the Maison Ardeber. Giant cement mixers were painstakingly conveyed down rue du Port, and sections of the coastline now were closed off to civilians. We could see, towering at the end of Grande Plage, a metallic installation for the extraction of gravel at low tide—the cement mixers were never still.

Much as we still liked Edgar Allan Poe, our favorite books were now *Robinson Crusoe* and Jules Verne's *The Mysterious Island*. These were stories of survival on deserted islands, they were about us. In our daily life there was the same suspense, the same camaraderie, and that particular, rounded feeling which an island gives and which I was savoring at that moment atop the jetty. La Rochelle appeared like an opalescent vision blurred by distance—not at all like a powder keg about to blow up under the Allies' bombs.

The sea now fed us. My father often went spearfishing with Colonel Merle, bringing back fat silvery mullets, which my grandmother cooked in the Provençal manner with a laurel leaf and small carrots. Sometimes they caught rays. These, with their sharklike heads, their long tails, and their fleshy wings, were straight out of *Twenty Thousand Leagues Under the Sea*.

Our procurement of dolphin was also out of Jules Verne. The Germans used dolphins as moving targets for their practice shooting. Once in a while, their freshly killed corpses washed up onto the beach, bleeding profusely. Even the hardened Oléronais said that it was cruel to kill these animals whose frolicking suggests a friendly spirit: they are the mythical animals who carry shipwrecked mariners to safety. Encouraged by Colonel Merle, who had eaten dolphin meat in his youth, we overcame our squeamishness and found that dolphin was rather like steak if properly trimmed.

The dolphin blubber was turned into a smooth transparent oil. Cut in small pieces, the blubber was rendered for a long time over a slow fire in our kitchen. That operation filled the Maison Ardeber with the stench so eloquently described in *Moby Dick*.

This had to be: our electric current was often shut off by the Germans. We burned the dolphin oil in small containers with homemade wicks, like the lamps used by early Christians in the catacombs. Their light was just bright enough to read by. To Julien's amusement, my grandmother also concocted an excellent hand cream using dolphin oil as a base, adding to it wild mint and chamomile, along with certain secret ingredients. This bit of witchcraft struck him as wondrously barbaric.

After much mock dismay, Julien, a gourmand, came to appreciate the squid prepared by the Chernushkis. It was cooked with my father's tomatoes and garlic and a dash of saffron Vera Kalita had given to my grandmother for Easter. What caused Julien to put on an act of fastidiousness was the fact that the squid was picked up on the beach, freshly killed by the other fish that hunt it in the shallow waters along the beach. Julien admired my father's imaginative approach to survival. Nothing in his own upbringing prepared him for such deeds as the carving of a dead dolphin on the beach, yet he was capable of great daring. He would often bicycle all the way to Méray after the curfew, eluding the German patrols in the dark. This terrified his mother, but there was no reasoning with him.

Aunt Natasha loved the sea almost as much as my father. She could swim far out into the ocean, staying in the water forever. Solidly but gracefully built, on the beach she looked like a sea goddess. When she decided that she would leave the Maison Ardeber to enable André to study in a lycée on the mainland, I was heartbroken—she was a vital participant in our romantic, shipwrecked existence on Oléron. I was going to miss her more than André. With Paul's arrival, a split had occurred between my cousin and myself that had not been mended.

The decision was taken in the summer of 1943: my aunt

was moving to Niort, a small southwestern town just outside the Atlantic wall. It was accessible from Paris, and my Uncle Daniel could visit his family there regularly. Niort had a good lycée.

By 1943, at thirteen, André, Paul, and I had graduated from the Ecole Communale of our village. There was no further course of studies available to us on the island. Paul was going off to La Rochelle to board at the lycée there. For a time it was thought that I might go on to Niort with Natasha, but my mother vetoed this. Instead, members of the family would tutor me in history and English. The rest, it was felt, could be made up through reading. Mathematics and Latin were postponed until better times.

There had been an attempt on the part of my grandmother to persuade the curé to give me Latin lessons. The curé had first agreed—eventually he declined. I was thirteen, past what was known as *l'âge canonique:* I could not come into unchaperoned contact with him. The story of my irrepressible grandmother—*cette étonnante* Madame Chernov—calling on the curé and discussing with him what constituted *l'âge canonique* became one of Madame Lutin's favorite tales. My grandmother's determination in taking on the curé, known throughout the island for his toughness, filled Julien's mother with delight.

Paul Rittoni's baptism into the Catholic faith took place just before Natasha and her boys left for Niort. It was a great event in Saint-Denis. It turned out that Paul, the son of a socialist mother, had not been baptized as an infant. Now he had completed a private course of religious studies with the red-faced curé and was ready to receive the Sacrament. The godfather would be none other than Colonel Bourrade, while Mademoiselle Charles had agreed to be his godmother.

To be presented to the world as an intimate of the Bourrade family was a triumph for Clara. I was pleased. If the Bourrades were to befriend her, she might leave us alone. They would lend her greater respectability than even my grandmother could. They were active in a variety of Pétainist good works; their daughters were organizing a Catholic youth club, rallying the local young peasants under the church banner with a program of sports and amateur theatricals.

But Clara still needed us as an audience before which she reenacted her successes at the Bourrades—at their birthday parties, at a dinner given in her honor. As might be expected, the colonel was secretly in love with her. War in Russia, once the main topic of Clara's conversation, was losing its appeal—in 1943 the Germans were beginning to eulogize the merits of what Hitler called the "elastic strategy."

Paul's baptism took place in our church one soft gray Sunday afternoon. My grandmother, Natasha, and André attended. I stayed home, but afterward I asked André many questions. To my cousin's disappointment, Paul was not immersed bodily in holy water; a symbolic sprinkling on the top of his head had sufficed. The ceremony was attended by the local bourgeoisie led by the Bourrades—no representative of the peasant families of Saint-Denis had come. In Paul's honor, Mademoiselle Charles had asked her confessor, the retired curé, to officiate while the new curé served as an attendant. The ceremony went smoothly although the old curé, a bit shaky, kept forgetting Paul's name.

The only difficulty came when the ancient leatherbound baptismal register had to be signed. The pen, which lay next to a half-empty inkwell, had refused to work. When Mademoiselle Charles made a large ink spot on the register, everyone became concerned, looking around for another pen. The new curé took over. *"Il faut lui casser les reins"*—"We must break its back—" he declared, breaking the old pen in two with a decisive gesture. Then he produced a black shiny fountain pen out of the deep folds of his soutane. The register was signed by everyone present, and Paul became a member of the Catholic church.

One aspect of this ceremony became a favorite subject of gossip during the *vendanges* that year: the Kalitas had not been invited to Paul's baptism. This was an affront: *l'Autrichienne* and *le Russe,* who both worked for the Germans, were no longer allies. Perhaps Clara, a protégée of the Bourrades, could no longer associate with dubious characters like the Kalitas. I do not know to this day the exact reason for their disaffection. Could sexual rejection by one or the other have poisoned their relationship? I suspect that they were both too calculating to let such a thing influence them. Perhaps Clara was becoming jealous of Kalita's infringement on her prerogatives as the Germans' only official translator. Clara liked to appear in the role of an inspired peacemaker, but Kalita would often quietly resolve some routine litigation just as she was getting ready to step forth and save everyone, like a new Joan of Arc.

Clara now found Madame Kalita *collante* ("sticky"), which is to say, a possessive bore. Indeed, Vera Kalita's dependence on Clara and Paul was extraordinary. She grieved and sought comfort through confidential chats with my grandmother whenever one or the other failed to visit her. And she took what Clara considered to be an undue interest in her personal affairs.

One day Clara failed to appear at a tea for two to which she had been summoned by Madame Kalita for what Russians call a "clarification of relations." Madame Kalita had baked a cake and made a pot of real tea, but her guest did not come that afternoon—nor ever again. Clara refused to see Vera and Andrei Kalita from that day on. She stopped recognizing them on the street, she forbade Paul to speak to them. My grandmother took Clara's side: Madame Kalita was maudlin. The task of comforting her fell to my mother, but Madame Kalita was inconsolable, while a deadly hatred was born between Clara Rittoni and Andrei Kalita.

Not long before that, a sweeping law had been passed in France under pressure from the Germans. The STO, the Service du Travail Obligatoire, made all Frenchmen from eighteen to sixty eligible for work in Germany. To make this acceptable to French public opinion, a highly publicized movement known as *La Relève* ("The Replacement") was instituted. For each Frenchman volunteering for Germany, a French prisoner of war—there were more than three million of them in Germany—would be repatriated. *La Relève* was of course fraudulent. Two or three thousand prisoners in ill health were sent home with enormous fanfare, while more than six hundred thousand young Frenchmen went off to work in Germany. In addition to this, by 1942, hundreds of thousands more were serving the Reich on French soil.

The peasants of Oléron were not sent off to Germany because they were useful on the island to the Reich's economy. However, all Frenchmen between eighteen and sixty were to work on the Atlantic wall two weeks out of every month. This was a hardship for the peasants, whose ranks had been thinned in 1939, but the women of Oléron were hard-working and the vineyards of Oléron continued to flourish.

Because the decree had said specifically *all Frenchmen,* Clara had been able to get Andrei Kalita out of working for the Germans. Kalita was not a French citizen, but a Russian refugee like my father, and the Germans were legalistic in their interpretation of their own texts. When he learned of Kalita's dispensation, my father had called on the Secretary of the Mairie, Monsieur Dupeux. He pointed out to him that he, too, was a Russian refugee. The secretary, who was said to be anti-German, decided that if Kalita had been exempted, so might my father, "with all these children to feed."

Now Clara brought to the attention of the German authorities the fact that able-bodied Russians were escaping the local draft through a technicality. Being Russian was no recommendation in France in 1943, and my father and Kalita were summoned to work at once. Monsieur Dupeux himself brought the summons to my father. Indignantly, he said that Madame Rittoni had made it impossible for the municipality to provide him with a dispensation. My father had to report two weeks hence at the gravel-extracting site on Grande Plage.

When Kalita received a similar order from Monsieur Dupeux, he was outraged. Andrei Kalita was of a choleric disposition. He was known to throw his plate of noodles against the wall whenever his wife's seasoning displeased him. On that day, Vera Kalita had feared that her husband might have apoplexy: he had just had a big lunch—one of Kalitas' own ducklings with cabbage. Recovering his self-control, Kalita offered a glass of wine to Monsieur Dupeux and coaxed him into telling him exactly what had happened. Then he jumped on his bicycle and sped on to Côte Sauvage.

As a purveyor of wine and cognac for the military, Kalita had free access to the batteries around Saint-Denis. Captain

Fink, the commanding officer on Côte Sauvage, was one of his customers. Shocked to hear what had happened, the captain picked up the telephone and had a few words with Colonel Wolff, the new commandant of Saint-Denis, an elderly, dour Prussian who had just arrived in the village. Not yet subjugated by Clara's charm, Colonel Wolff authorized the captain to issue a document exempting Andrei Kalita from working on the Atlantic wall "because of his usefulness to the Occupation armies."

Kalita bicycled back to Saint-Denis in triumph, going straight to the Mairie. He gave his document to Monsieur Dupeux, who congratulated him on his good fortune. But the paper was in German and Monsieur Dupeux had to have a copy of it in French. He asked Madame Rittoni to translate it. Unknown to anyone, Clara kept a duplicate of Kalita's exemption; yet the only immediate consequence of her aggression against Kalita was to force my father to spend half his working hours on the construction of the Atlantic wall.

Volodia

Uncle Volodia's arrival on Oléron, in 1943, and Julien's departure are fused in my mind as one memory, involving that dark land, Germany, which was now the target of devastating bombardments. At that time, the pace of our existence was accelerating. The feeling that we were experiencing eternity rather than life was fading. We were again moving forward, toward that mysterious future I thought I had seen in the darkness at the end of the curving lane past Clara's house.

Julien's departure—not being a peasant, he was draftable for Germany—plunged me into sorrow, but at the same time, it made my life easier. Year after year it was torture to be without news from him for long stretches of time while knowing that he was only seven kilometers away. I was still as infatuated with him as I was with the world of French literature he had brought into our life, but obscurely I realized that Julien belonged forever to Madame Lutin alone, though at the time he was causing her only tribulations. Julien was constantly getting involved in daredevil adventures. Delicate physically, he was nonetheless capable of swimming in the middle of a raging storm, or entering a mine field to pick a blue thistle. The fact that the Occupation was becoming harsher, with rigorous curfew hours and night patrols, only provoked him to more nightly wanderings.

When the STO caught up with him, Madame Lutin remained stoical. She was already in mourning—Madame Duval had died not long before. It was said on the island that Madame Lutin's mother had died of grief caused by the French defeat.

As for Maître Lutin, he tried to persuade himself and everyone around him that going off to Germany was salutary for Julien, that it would help him mature. The *notaire* continued to drop by at the Maison Ardeber on Wednesdays to have a cup of linden tea before bicycling back to Méray, a long trip for a man of his age. Sipping his tea, he went on about how *"Les voyages forment la jeunesse,"* and what amusing letters Julien was sending home from Düsseldorf, where he worked as a street sweeper—Julien was in fact a grave digger there. The Allies' bombardments all over Europe, and especially over Germany, were becoming apocalyptic.

Uncle Volodia's return from Germany was one of those happy events of which there are only a few in a lifetime. The letters he wrote from Germany describing his daily encounters and thoughts had made his presence vividly felt even before his arrival. So did the anguished dream I sometimes had about him, in which he was looking for us in that twilight land, Germany. When we learned, through a telegram, that because of a persistent hernia he was one of the rare beneficiaries of "The Replacement," it had seemed both wondrous and natural. Volodia belonged to Oléron.

Volodia was tall, slender, and had limpid blue eyes. Despite the years of hard work in a labor camp he had retained his military bearing—one that failed to disguise his almost extravagant kindness. I adored him for his playful, energizing presence and for his sense of chivalry, which, unlike my father's, was a bit theatrical, yet completely authentic.

Volodia had presents for all of us—making these by hand was a favorite pastime for inmates in camps. There was a cigarette lighter for Vadim, a ring for Ariadne, and handbound notebooks for the Chernushkis. For me, he had a magnificent gift which had been traded for one of his own handicrafts. It is still in my possession, a German art book entitled *Painters of the Renaissance*. For the first time I saw Giorgione's *Venus* and Botticelli's *Primavera* in reproduction. They were a revelation; I resolved to become a painter when I grew up.

For days on end, Volodia told us about what had happened to him since we had last seen him. He had started in Alsace, where most of his foreign legion battalion was destroyed in 1940. He had been taken prisoner by the Germans three times in a row; each time he had escaped and each time he was recaptured. In Germany, the best of the French working-class spirit had flourished in his camp—it was a soldiers' camp, not an officers'. My uncle, who had never known any French people intimately until the war, was now enamored of the French popular virtues—the French *bonne humeur*, the French *camaraderie*, the French *débrouillardise* ("ability to manage").

There were stories which Volodia told only after we children had gone to bed. Since Clara had moved out, I shared with my grandmother the salon next to the dining room and overheard them. There was another camp in proximity to his own, where Russian prisoners of war were dying of cold and hunger by the thousands. Their corpses were removed and other Russians were brought in, and when these died, more came. A French "solidarity committee," which Volodia had helped organize in his camp, had tried to aid the dying, collecting supplies among the French prisoners of war and smuggling them to the Russians, but nothing could save them.

One evening Volodia, lowering his voice even more—though I could still hear him—said that yet more sinister camps existed in the depths of German and Polish forests. These housed Jews from all over Europe, the hundreds of thousands who had "left without leaving an address" after their arrest by the gestapo. No one knew what went on in these camps—but it had to be fearsome. My uncle was determined to go to work for the French Resistance. He and my father had long conversations on the subject in muffled voices late into the night.

Clara, who visited us less often since she had been befriended by the Bourrades, reappeared at our house when Volodia arrived. My uncle was pleased: in the beginning of his captivity, in letters from home, he had been told that Paul was acting as an affectionate older brother to Aliosha, and that Clara was especially attentive to Ariadne. Arriving at our house on the day of Volodia's return, Clara declared that my uncle had always been her favorite in our family. "Such a chivalrous, beautiful man!" she kept repeating, looking at him admiringly. She asked Volodia about his fighting in the foreign legion and listened to him with total absorption. She did not say a word about herself, nor her work at the Kommandantur.

Volodia was bewildered: everyone in our family seemed to have reservations about Clara. The exceptions were my grandmother, as beguiled as ever, and Ariadne, who remained aloof, retreating behind the impassiveness which was her mask whenever family conflicts involving her mother threatened to arise. What had happened? How could anyone be cold to this angelic woman? What about Vadim, this most generous of men?

The young Chernushkis and my father remained reticent, but that evening my grandmother made an announcement. The cooling of our friendship with the Rittonis was caused principally by little Olga's difficult disposition. She did not get along with people, she was disagreeable to Clara and to the Kalitas. Unchecked by her parents, she had driven Clara and Paul away from the Maison Ardeber.

This was the only direct confrontation my grandmother and I were ever to have on the subject of Clara. Although we lived in close quarters in the salon and got along excellently on a day-to-day basis, we never discussed her. We knew that neither of us would change her mind about Clara. That evening, faced with a sudden, public denunciation, I felt betrayed. I thought that I had shown great restraint by never challenging or ridiculing my grandmother's infatuation. The notion that I could not get along with people cut me to the quick. My mother took my defense: Clara was at times very self-absorbed.

My grandmother emphatically disagreed: Clara was selflessness personified, sacrificing herself for the good of the community. An argument ensued. But everyone in our family was too gallant, or perhaps too prudish, to bring up the one fact that was then the talk of Saint-Denis and had to be known to the adults. In school I had heard girls discussing the crucial question, "*La tarpette se couche-t-elle avec les Allemands?*" ("Does the interpreter sleep with the Germans?") No one knew for certain, but people were on the alert for clues. And Clara, who might never have gone to bed with a German, could not resist showing off the devotion she inspired. At dusk in the good season, along the lane near Mademoiselle Charles's house, one could see the silhouette of some German officer gazing up at her as she leaned gracefully out of her window, like Juliet, her blond hair undone.

However, soon afterward, Volodia was to witness the intrigue which resulted in my father's requisition for work on the Atlantic wall. It put an end to Clara's visits to the Maison Ardeber. This was fortunate, for no ripple of excitement, no matter how slight, ever escaped Clara, and by 1943, my father had at last succeeded in contacting a Resistance network on the mainland.

That year I sensed that something unusual was going on in our house. Colonel Merle came by at odd hours, looking for my father and Volodia. Monsieur Guyonnet, the schoolmaster, would drop by and wait for my father's return from his fields, reminiscing about past Socialist congresses with my grandmother. When my father came home, the two of them would go down to the jetty to watch the sunset. One day, an unknown man, who looked like a fisherman in thigh-high rubber boots and a blue woolen cap, came by. He accepted a cup of barley coffee from my grandmother, then he dashed across the street to Colonel Merle's house and was seen no more.

By 1943 our friendship with Colonel Merle was very close. In the absence of his wife and children, he had adopted us. He would drop by in the evenings and regale us with slightly off-color stories about his garrison years. He shared with us the latest village gossip. Having been brought up on Oléron, he knew everyone on the island. He told us the nicknames of our neighbors: mustachioed Madame Braud across the street was *le*

Hussard; Monsieur Masson, Mademoiselle Charles's cousin, who waved his long arms as he told people about the need for a second jetty in Saint-Denis, was *Moulin à Vent*.

We, too, often crossed the street to the colonel's house at night. Behind heavy wooden shutters we listened to Radio London on his receiver. It was not strong enough to catch Radio Moscow but, since the curfew hours had been moved back to eight and then to seven, going to the Kalitas had become more difficult, although we risked it on moonless nights for the sake of hearing news in Russian. Whenever we went to Colonel Merle's in the evenings, the Chernushkis would take along for him, in a small milkcan, a portion of the vegetable soup which we had had for dinner. Although he was a famed gardener, who competed with my father for the earliest tomatoes in Saint-Denis, Colonel Merle was no cook.

By now my father's gardens were reaching their peak, providing ample provisions for all of us throughout the year. They had been reorganized to make a harmonious whole. The year before, Monsieur Masson had put the vast, walled-in orchard at the back of our house at our disposal. In exchange, in the summer my father was to give him the vegetables and fruit he needed. The orchard of the old Charles estate had been neglected for years, but under my father's care it soon became a garden of Eden.

Behind its high walls, the garden was sheltered from the destructive northwestern wind of Oléron, the Norua. Tobacco and strawberries flourished there at the earliest possible time in the spring. The fruit trees around it were of choice varieties. Four kinds of apples grew there—pale yellow *calvilles*, green cooking apples, brown *reinettes*, and golden ones, and the classic red apple out of French fairy tales, which looks like the American red delicious. These could be kept through the winter in one of the armoires at the Maison Ardeber. They filled the house with a faint flowery smell.

But the greatest virtue of Monsieur Masson's garden was its privacy. With an enormous stone well in its middle, with neatly laid out alleys and several flat stones disposed as benches in its sunnier spots, the garden was orderly and secluded. Its walls were at least four meters high and its gate resembled that of a medieval fortress, strengthened with wrought iron crossbars and latches. The garden was a sanctuary, the most sheltering spot in all of Saint-Denis. The treasure we had been looking for in Mademoiselle Charles's grove was surely buried there, and we intended to start digging for it at the earliest opportunity.

With Natasha, André, and Kiska gone, we were now without the small monthly money order sent to us by Daniel. Fortunately, everyone in the village was becoming tolerant of debts: on Oléron there was a heightened feeling of danger, and solidarity was beginning to grow even among the individualistic islanders. "We trust you, you'll pay us back after the war!" Madame Bouchat would say whenever we picked up our bread rations, as she made one more entry in the special notebook where our debt was consigned. Mademoiselle Charles came by one day to tell my grandmother that we no longer needed to pay the rent, at least not until *des temps meilleurs*. "You'll reimburse my cousin Ardeber—in better times," she said. People spoke a lot about better times, past and future.

To raise a little cash, we tried collecting a seaweed known on Oléron by its medieval name, *goémon*. It grew on rocks far out to sea and could only be gathered at very low tide. At the time, it was in demand for the production of gelatin: *goémon* in its dried, bleached form was used as a food substitute in what was called then the "ersatz industry."

Our whole family went *goémon*-gathering during the huge equinox tides of Oléron. Curly brown seaweed was pulled off the rocks by hand, then it was stuffed into old flour sacks borrowed from Monsieur Bouchat. This had to be done quickly because of the rapidly rising tide. The feeling that the sea might carry us away was scary yet exhilarating. We hurried back to the shore, dragging along the weighty sacks buoyed by the incoming water. We took them to the Masson garden in the *remorque*, the small two-wheeled carriage put together by my father from parts of worn-out bicycles and old planks.

The bags of seaweed were clumsy, and they left a trail of seawater and sand on the pavement. The carriage squeaked as we pulled it up rue du Port and through the gates of Monsieur Masson's garden. There, the *goémon* was spread evenly on the grass around the fruit trees. Sun and rain bleached the fleshy, sleek seaweed, turning it brittle and feather-light in a matter of days. Then it was sold to a dealer from Le Château. A kilo went for the equivalent of five dollars, but it took a gigantic amount of *goémon* to make up that weight.

Soon Volodia started looking for a job on the island, one that would not strain his health. Perhaps because of his croix de guerre, he was hired as an accountant at the Cooperative Vinicole, a community-operated winery producing the region's greatest specialty, cognac. The Cooperative Vinicole was a large ramshackle building located on the southern edge of Saint-Pierre. Within walking distance from it, along the highway, the Sossinskys were allocated an old windmill as lodgings. They moved there in the beginning of 1944.

Moulin du Coivre was a perfectly preserved nineteenth-century windmill. The wooden skeleton of its great wings extended high into the air. Inside, its millstone and its whole wooden structure, including the hand-carved ladders and wheels, were intact. The mill was now used as a storage room; the Sossinskys lived in an adjoining farmhouse, primitive but stylish with its earthen floors. Outside stood a well topped by a graceful wrought-iron tripod.

There was an important advantage to the Sossinskys' move, which, at first, was not openly discussed by the adults. In Saint-Pierre contacts with the Resistance on the mainland would be less conspicuous. People could drop by the moulin unnoticed. Though it bordered on the highway, it was placed in such a way that nothing could be seen inside the yard formed by the mill, the well, and the farmhouse.

My grandmother was to divide her time between the Moulin and Maison Ardeber—this provided her with the movement she loved. Only the four Andreyevs now lived in Saint-Denis. Sasha and I became individuals, the son and daughter of our parents. This was enjoyable, but it was also lonely. At thirteen, I led the life of an adult. I daydreamed about having friends of my age. Young people—*les jeunes*—were in fashion under Pétain, yet there were no *jeunes* in our village outside of the pro-German club led by the Bourrade girls. I developed a friendship with Madame Marquet, the Kalitas' landlady.

She had been a pretty Parisienne dressmaker who had married a member of the bourgeoisie, a well-to-do stockbroker. The Marquets had retired to Saint-Denis just before the war. My friend, recently widowed, maintained that she was a medium in touch with the world of spirits. On evenings when they were well disposed, Châteaubriand and Alfred de Vigny dictated their new works to Madame Marquet. Sitting in the dark, she wrote these down in a special notebook. My grandmother once witnessed one of her seances and was impressed, but unfortunately Madame Marquet would not let me attend: "Petite Olga," she said, "you are too much of a skeptic. You'd intimidate the spirits."

Madame Marquet's salon was full of gilded chairs and sofas, plumply upholstered in mauve brocade. Her life-size portrait and that of Monsieur Marquet done in pastels hung there along with realistic studies of calla lilies and irises. Madame Marquet always dressed in black, but with a Parisian touch of refinement I appreciated. She smelled of Houbigant's "Quelques fleurs," which was said to capture the delicate odor of irises.

One of Madame Marquet's greatest attractions was her library full of naughty novels, risqué boulevard plays, and decadent turn-of-the-century poetry. Since I had no friends and no school to attend, I rewarded myself by reading these. I enjoyed their suggestive approach to sex, not to be found in the chaste Russian classics. Bedroom humor in the French style was frowned upon by my parents, but they did not interfere with my reading. My right to read anything I wanted, including the Marquis de Sade, had been established by my father some years before, much to my grandmother's dismay. De Sade was not to be found at Madame Marquet's—I had to content myself with Feydeau.

Now that we were a small family, my parents were candid about my father's Resistance activities. Recently, Kalita had been taken in as a member of the small local cell. There had been a request from the mainland for plans of the German batteries around the island, and Kalita was the only civilian besides Clara who had had access to these. Since my father had trusted him enough to introduce him into the Resistance, I made up my mind that the Kalitas were acceptable, although I continued to harbor reservations about them and their white terrier, Bebka. All three struck me as frivolous. In 1943, despite my risqué reading, I was very high-minded.

The proposal to ambush German soldiers or to blow up German equipment, made by my father, Colonel Merle, and several others in Saint-Denis, had for the time being been emphatically denied by the leaders of the Resistance, who were determined to avoid the horrendous reprisals that had resulted elsewhere from terrorist acts against the Occupation armies. My father and Colonel Merle were like two restive adolescents. The idea that the Germans might be defeated without their participation was maddening to them and also to my grandmother, an activist by temperament. She and the colonel had heated discussions on the subject. My grandmother even put up with the fact that the colonel called Clara *cette garce* ("that hussy") within her hearing. In her eyes, Clara, a saint sacrificing herself for the sake of others, was tragically misjudged. My grandmother was certain that Clara would one day be publicly vindicated.

The Russians from Russia

Julien had gone off to Germany in a jacket made by Madame Lutin from a World War I army blanket of the *notaire*'s, while my father wore a plaid one cut out of a moth-eaten lap robe given to us by the Lutins. Despite the Chernushkis' skill as seamstresses—they had the Russian instinctive costume-making talents—we had begun to look like a family of gypsies. This look was highlighted by the red bandanna my father wore to work summer and winter.

Clara had long objected to this bandanna, warning us that it attracted the Germans' attention. They were asking ominous questions "about that tall swarthy man in the red kerchief working alone in his fields." Recently, Colonel Wolff had pointedly inquired why this *White* Russian insisted on wearing a *red* bandanna. On the early February morning when my father went off for the first time to work for the Germans, my mother persuaded him at the last minute to trade the provocative bandanna for Volodia's old beret.

At the gravel-extracting installation, about ten men from the village were at work under the leadership of a German corporal. German soldiers armed with rifles supervised them. A primitive motor hauled a half-dozen rusty ore cars loaded with gravel up the beach; these were emptied into a truck. Using shovels, the Frenchmen standing at the water's edge were filling the ore cars with wet gravel, getting sprayed whenever a wave broke at their feet.

The spirit of good fellowship that prevailed among the Frenchmen made working at the gravel-extracting installation tolerable for my father. Everyone on the team was anti-German. There was incessant, veiled joking about the Germans' persistence in planting "Rommel's asparagus stalks," the pine tree trunks linked by barbed wire that were to prevent the Allies from landing on our beaches. The trunks were forever being uprooted by the tides, and certain enterprising Oléronais collected them for firewood behind the Germans' backs. Rommel, the alleged inventor of this device, was now one of the two commanders-in-chief along the Atlantic wall.

The Germans supervising the Frenchmen's work were middle-aged, taciturn men who were not, as a rule, aggressive. They sensed that a confrontation was imminent and they did not wish to antagonize the future adversary. News was bad for Germany that year. Mussolini had fallen from power, and now the Allies were conquering Italy from the south.

For the most part, the men holding Oléron were not Germans at all but belonged to other European nationalities. The officers were still Germans, but they were no longer clipped, assertive Prussians. These men had experienced defeat in the North African desert or in Russia; they had suffered wounds and military humiliation. For them, Oléron was a haven, and they wanted it to endure. Keeping an eye on them, a few SS officers had made their appearance on the island.

The spectacular fortifications of the Atlantic wall created the impression that the Germans would hold forever the coasts of France. Yet that spring, once again the ocean was asserting itself as our master. Oléron's name is said to be derived from an ancient English nautical term, "All run," an injunction to sailors to bypass at full speed an area marked by hazardous shoals and currents. And indeed, the force of the ocean around Oléron can be wondrous. It began dismantling the German fortifications even before their completion. On the beach, we found evidence of British vessels wrecked nearby—useful things like English-made light bulbs, aluminum saucepans, and lemons, which we had not tasted for years. If there was to be a landing, the ocean would decide its outcome: despite the sea mines disposed along the coast, despite the huge cement mixers and the hundreds of thousands of kilometers of barbed wire woven about its every dune, Oléron would not be tamed.

One day in early 1944, during my father's second stretch of duty at the gravel-extracting site, an argument started between a Frenchman and a German soldier. The men had no common language, and the hatred between them flared. As the Frenchmen looked on, the German was waving his revolver at the peasant. My father, who usually tried to play down his knowledge of German, offered to interpret. Summoned by one of the guards, a sergeant came down to the beach. He spoke in an accommodating manner: the incident was settled.

The German sergeant, who turned out to be an Austrian, offered my father a cigarette, which he accepted after a second's hesitation. The Austrian told my father about his feelings for

Oléron. "Such a peaceful, patriarchal island! After the forests of Briansk . . ." Then he asked my father who he was. Upon hearing that my father was Russian, the Austrian said that he had great respect for the Russian people. "How courageous! And how they love their country, so bleak compared to this island, or to our mountains in Austria." As he was leaving, the Austrian added: "By the way, do you know that there are several Russians here on the island, serving in the Wehrmacht? I have one of them, a boy of seventeen, in my battery nearby, at La Morelière. The poor boy is so lost! I am fond of him; I could be his father. I'll send him down to talk to you. It might cheer him to be able to speak some Russian. I am afraid he may kill himself—he is so homesick."

A few minutes later a young soldier walked down the dune with long, lanky steps. He was tall and had brilliant green eyes. To hear this fair young soldier in German uniform introduce himself as Misha Dudin in Russian marked with a Ukrainian accent was a shock for my father, who remained quiet. The young man, too, said nothing for a time, standing mournfully on the wet sand. My father had stopped shoveling gravel and looked at the boy. Suddenly the Russian's eyes filled with tears. "I understand," he said in a soft voice, and he plucked at the sleeve of his gray green military tunic. "Believe me, I feel awful about it."

My father tried to be as friendly as he could with Misha Dudin, telling him his own name and patronymic, and explaining that he was an exile who had but one desire—to go back to Russia one day. Though he remembered Volodia's tales about the Russian death camp, he could not get over the sight of Misha's uniform. Misha sensed this and started to leave. My father asked him to come by the gravel-extracting site again. He had believed the boy when he had said that he and his comrades, the other Russians on the island, had had no choice but to put on a German uniform or die. "How will we ever erase this shame?" he had said gloomily, plucking at the sleeve of his tunic.

Two days later, the young man again came down to the gravel-extracting site. My father could not help but be charmed by his soulfulness and his beautiful green eyes. Misha was happy because two other Russians—"good men who, no matter how it looked to others, loved their country"—had been assigned to his platoon. The following Sunday afternoon they would have a leave; Misha Dudin wanted to know whether he and his two friends could stop by our house for a conversation—to explain "how it was that they were wearing these clothes, which burned their skin as if they were made of fire."

My father was hesitant: he proposed a meeting on the beach instead. "We would not embarrass you by coming to your house in our German uniforms," Misha Dudin said, "but it would not be good for us to be seen together here. The Germans are suspicious. Few are like our Austrian sergeant, who saved my life when I was ready to hang myself on my German leather belt. They fear us." My father gave in and explained to him how to find our house on rue du Port. Misha Dudin, with his clear eyes, could not be a provocateur.

But the following Sunday no Russians in or out of German uniform appeared at the Maison Ardeber, although we waited for them anxiously. I was dying of curiosity at the prospect of meeting Russians from Russia—not émigrés like all the other Russians I had known. The only other Russian from today's Russia I had ever met was Isaac Babel.

On Monday, Misha Dudin appeared for a minute at the

gravel-extracting works: he and his friends had been deprived of their outing because of an argument they had had with a German corporal. They hoped for better luck on the following Sunday.

But my father, who had urgent spring planting to finish in Monsieur Masson's garden, did not stay home on that next Sunday. Only my mother, Sasha, and I were at the Maison Ardeber—my grandmother was spending the week in Saint-Pierre. As always, since my aunts and their families had moved away, the house seemed unnaturally quiet. My mother and I were writing letters. Sasha was playing in the garden. He had wanted to go to Monsieur Masson's garden with my father but the day was too chilly for that.

I will never forget Sasha's face as he rushed into the dining room where we were settled at the round table. He said in a low voice: "There are soldiers in the garden—and they speak *Russian!*" He was seven, an intense child with thick blond hair and a small round, serious face. Sasha was full of fire. He adored my father. Whenever he went to Monsieur Masson's garden with him, he dragged a huge Ardeber mattock along the pavement on rue du Port. It clanged and made sparks and Sasha said with solemnity: *"Sasha et Vadim sont de grands ouvriers"* ("Sasha and Vadim are great workers").

Sasha knew all about the great battles of Russia: Kiev, Briansk, Orel, Stalingrad. He could find these cities on the map that was locked in a desk drawer in my grandmother's room.

Standing in the doorway, he was now observing the Russians in the garden. He was oblivious to the fact that they were wearing German uniforms. The Russians, too, seemed transfixed. My mother quickly ushered them into the dining room. Fortunately, it was the early part of the afternoon on a

Sunday, and rue du Port was empty. My mother sent Sasha to fetch his father. Sasha exclaimed excitedly: "Yes, I'll go get Papa right away!"

The oldest of the three men could not contain himself. "A Russian boy! His name is Sasha—and he speaks *Russian!*" he cried out, and pulling a handkerchief out of his pocket, he blew his nose.

The three soldiers in black boots and holsters with pistols dwarfed our dining room—they themselves were aware of their own upsetting appearance. My mother asked them to sit down. They declined: "Let us wait for the host," the oldest man said in a formal manner. We all stood up while my mother introduced herself as Olga Victrovna. Then she presented me and asked the names of our visitors. In addition to Misha Dudin, whom I found even more beautiful than my father had described him— the color of his eyes against his golden skin was an astonishing light green—there was a second young man in the group. Leva was broad-shouldered and had a wide, squarish face. He did not smile, and he spoke slowly and thoughtfully.

The third man was about my father's age, in his late thirties. He was short and bony, with graying hair and a suntanned, wrinkled face. When he introduced himself as Ivan Petrovich, I was struck by his courtly manner and the melodiousness of his speech. Was this how Russians from Russia spoke? My mother and I looked at each other, and each knew what the other was thinking. Surely my father's new acquaintance, Misha Dudin, was right, and he and his friends had to be "good men" despite their uniforms.

When my father arrived with Sasha, the soldiers took off the heavy leather holsters with the pistols and threw them in a heap in a corner of the room. Then we sat down and my mother and I served linden tea with tiny glasses of cognac, which were drunk ceremoniously. Sasha sat first at the table on a separate chair, but after a while he curled up in Ivan Petrovich's lap. He was spellbound.

Thinking back to that day, I find it remarkable that our visitors made no inquiry about how *we* felt about the Germans. I suppose that my parents' reaction to their uniforms had answered this question before it was asked. The Russians took turns telling us their stories, centered on what was evidently a dreadful wound—how it was that they, who loved their country, were now soldiers in the German army. All three men came from around Kiev. Of the three, Leva was the only one who had gone to high school. Misha spoke first—he was the most ebullient of the three.

In 1941, when he was only fourteen, Misha had been led away on foot from his small Ukrainian village. After almost a year of forced labor in a German armament factory, he was given the choice of putting on a German uniform or being sent to a camp. He had heard that Russian prisoners' camps were death camps—only those who worked there as camp officials survived. "I know I am a coward," Misha said. "I do love Russia, but it must be that I love life better, and so I put this on"—and again he pulled at the sleeve of his gray green tunic.

Now it was Leva's turn to speak. He was too young to be drafted when the war had broken out—he became a guerrilla instead. He was captured in the woods behind the German lines. With a group of Russian partisans he was led to an open mass grave and shot, but somehow he was only wounded. At night, he had crawled out of the pit full of corpses. He had lived in the forest, eating berries and raw mushrooms, hoping to cross the front and return to the Russian side. But the German advance toward Moscow had been so swift that he never caught up with the front. He was recaptured and treated as a war prisoner: by then he wore a Soviet uniform, which he had removed from a dead Russian. He was incorporated into a group of prisoners who were given a choice. They were to enlist as "volunteers" in the Wehrmacht or be shot on the spot. About one-third of the men refused to volunteer and were killed. Leva decided to "volunteer." "I consider myself condemned to death anyway," he said. "I think it is better that I stay alive a bit longer. This way, before I die, I can still hope to serve Russia."

Ivan Petrovich was taken prisoner near Kiev in the fall of 1941. Like hundreds of thousands of others, he was marched off to Germany from the Kiev region and assigned to a camp where the prisoners were dying of hunger and exposure. They were not put to work—except to bury the dead. As winter came, rags were thrown to them. These were worn-out German uniforms. By midwinter the rare survivors were dressed like "ghosts of Germans, in German rags," as Ivan Petrovich put it. "We were barely ourselves, barely human." Then one day a German lieutenant and an execution squad appeared at the camp. The lieutenant greeted the surviving Russians as "brave volunteers against Bolshevism." They were offered warm food and new German uniforms. Those who did not want to put these on could step aside and be shot on the spot—some of them were, but not many.

The Russians had been careful to relate their stories indirectly, because Sasha was listening to their every word. But despite the euphemisms, we were shattered. I remembered that during the battle of Stalingrad I had tried to imagine how the Russians who fought there looked, and could not. Now I did. I glanced at my parents. I think that they had made up their minds right then that the three men could not have been sent out by the Germans to trap us.

Concerned for Sasha, my mother tried to give another turn to the conversation. She asked the men about their relatives and related to them the story of our family—how it had been forced into exile first by the tzars and now by the Soviets. Indeed, the Russians seemed fascinated by the fate of Russians outside Russia. When my father told them about how bitter life was in the emigration, they looked surprised. In those years, the fact that he was unable to live in Russia seemed catastrophic to my father. He recounted how his godfather, the Russian writer Maxim Gorky, had, in a conversation with Stalin, obtained for him the promise of a reentry visa in 1935. Gorky's death shortly afterward had put an end to my father's hope of going home. The Russians were astonished to hear that Father was connected with Gorky—and had been the subject of an interview between him and Stalin. Ivan Petrovich may also have been surprised that someone would do the impossible to go back to Russia in 1935. Earlier he had said that his own parents had died far away from home, somewhere in Siberia, at about that time, but he did not elaborate.

The soldiers were evidently touched by my father's love of Russia, and by how Russian our family had remained despite a lifetime abroad. Ivan Petrovich sighed and blew his nose. Misha Dudin asked my parents whether they had any Russian books to lend them—Gorky's or anyone else's. My mother brought out the collected works of Lermontov and Dostoyevsky's *A Raw Youth*. Misha's and Leva's eyes shone—they had not seen a Russian book in years.

When the men were ready to leave, Ivan Petrovich asked my mother whether, as a farewell, he and his friends could sing us a song. And they did, in a mellow, ever so slightly mournful manner—the three were friends and used to singing together.

Keeping their voices down because of the neighbors, the soldiers sang the ancient "Poluyshko," and then, at my mother's request, a prerevolutionary convicts' song, "Baikal." It was as if Russia herself, with her suffering and her lyric beauty, had entered the Maison Ardeber.

As the Russians were reluctantly saying good-bye, I went to inspect rue du Port, now growing dusky, to make sure that it was empty. While Ivan Petrovich was hugging Sasha and Misha Dudin was taking leave of my mother, Leva led my father aside and asked him whether Vadim Leonidovich could put him and his friends in touch with the Resistance. That evening, my father's answer was noncommittal, but his inner conviction was that the three Russians could become useful to the French underground.

Armagnac

My grandmother spent most of that winter of 1943-44 at the Moulin du Coivre. The Maison Ardeber had become the realm of the Andreyevs. For a while we almost never saw Clara. By then my father and Volodia had made up their minds that our new Russian friends could be recruited into the Resistance. The three and a number of other Russians from around the island went to work for the mainland network, which had taken the name "Réseau Armagnac." They began establishing maps of the military installations on the island. The Russians drew detailed plans for the eventual destruction of ammunition depots and weaponry throughout Oléron.

Clara must have sensed that something extraordinary was going on. Suddenly her visits to us multiplied. She listened attentively to everything that was said. Fortunately, most encounters between my father and the Russians—there were now about fifteen of them involved—took place in the seclusion of Monsieur Masson's garden. The soldiers could reach it through the pines and fields without going into the village.

Clara was feverishly looking for Resistance connections, but for her these were proving elusive. Volodia and my father feigned ignorance when she pressed them with questions. My grandmother, on the other hand, was persuaded that her friend would be invaluable to the Réseau Armagnac. One day she tried to bring Clara together directly with Leva, a great favorite of hers.

Leva was assuming the informal leadership of the Russians active in helping the French Resistance—with his partisan training, he turned out to be a superb underground organizer. While, to my great satisfaction, Misha Dudin and Ivan Petrovich had remained in La Morelière near Saint-Denis, Leva had been assigned to a battery near the Moulin du Coivre called La Perroche.

My uncle's house had by then become the main center of the Armagnac network on the island. The nearby distillery, which was selling cognac to German soldiers, provided an excellent screen for the comings and goings of the Resistance sympathizers, whether French civilians or Russians in German uniform. The Sossinskys and my grandmother saw Leva almost every day. My grandmother decided to make arrangements for Leva to meet Clara in private.

The encounter that my grandmother had planned, without taking anyone into her confidence, was to occur near an old well on the outskirts of Saint-Pierre. However, on the given day, Leva simply did not appear at the designated spot. Clara decided that my grandmother's "Russian friend," if he existed at all, was of no consequence.

A few days after this nonmeeting, which had the adults greatly agitated when they heard of it—any kind of indiscretion could at that time have dreadful consequences for all of us and for Armagnac—a horse-drawn carriage appeared on rue du Port near Clara's lane. With everyone on rue du Port looking on, German soldiers loaded Clara's and Paul's belongings onto it. A week before, Paul had returned to Saint-Denis from boarding school in La Rochelle: the nightly air raids there were now relentless. The explosions could be heard in Saint-Denis day and night, a distant, endless summer thunder.

Within an hour the loaded carriage, with bicycles tied atop a heap of suitcases, had left rue du Port. Without saying goodbye to anyone, Clara and Paul rode away in a black automobile driven by a German. It was rumored in the village afterward that Clara had moved to Saint-Trojan, to the milder end of the island where the mimosas bloomed, but this was never verified.

Saint-Trojan, at the opposite end of the island, was worlds away from Saint-Denis.

Clara's departure left me elated. At that moment, our life on the island was becoming a breathtaking adventure. The dull fear experienced by those who are powerless to defend themselves had vanished. The romance and high deeds I thought I had seen as my fate at the end of Clara's lane were coming true.

The Russians on Oléron were giving me, for the first time in my life, a sense of myself. I felt strength, which was to carry me through the following year, and the years afterward. It seemed that until then, since my early childhood, I had been explaining myself to strangers, fearing that I might otherwise remain forever unidentified, an oddity, a girl without a country. Emigrés were always looking at the children of fellow émigrés with melancholy eyes, noticing how badly they spoke Russian, how Gallic their manners. The French, on the other hand, deplored one's peculiar, non-French ways.

But the Russians on Oléron, like those other Russians whom I was to meet some fifteen years later in Moscow and Leningrad, regarded me as one of them, although I did speak Russian with a trace of an accent. Meeting them was to mark Sasha as well for the rest of his life—more intensely so because he was so young.

In those days, to my astonishment I was finding that I had to avoid lonely trips to the beach because some smiling German soldier, who was as likely as not to be an Italian or a Czech, would appear in a matter of minutes and try to engage me in conversation. To be a pretty girl was no more than a disguise, an unexpected role to play as well as possible, and I loved it. I had a great friendship with Misha Dudin. If I so much as glanced at him or asked him which poem by Lermontov he liked best, he seemed delighted. He was so innocent-looking that the Germans treated him as a pet and left him quite free in his movements. He often dropped by the Maison Ardeber at odd hours. To be with him was more fun than to try and fail to capture Julien's attention.

I still thought constantly about Julien, alone in a bombed-out Düsseldorf. Once in a while some Wehrmacht soldier, like that Austrian who had spoken with my father at the gravel works, would allow that Germany was under a rain of fire, that it was becoming an inferno.

Whenever we bicycled from Saint-Denis to Saint-Pierre, I urged my mother to stop by the Lutins' house in Méray. There had been no news from Julien since May, which was blamed by the *notaire* on nothing more than postal irregularities. An outwardly cheerful Madame Lutin would serve us a cup of tea in the dining room, which smelled of fresh wax. The *notaire* would come in for a chat. He no longer made speeches about the necessity for Frenchmen to learn to discipline themselves. The *notaire*'s house, without Madame Duval and Julien there, looked funereal. The house in Méray, the island, our entire existence— all were ruled by unknown, menacing laws. Anything could happen, as in a story by Edgar Allan Poe, yet on Oléron that year I felt free.

A period of intense activity started at the Maison Ardeber. Through Volodia, every week, the military information gathered at our end of the island was conveyed to the mainland. It would have been unsafe for Volodia, and for my father—men of draftable age who spoke French with a pronounced Russian accent—to go frequently between Saint-Denis and Saint-Pierre, but whenever the women in our family ventured back and forth it went unnoticed, having the appearance of routine family visiting.

Every week or two I rode to Saint-Pierre on my father's bicycle. If there were maps or diagrams to carry, they were sewn inside an old stuffed toy tied to the baggage rack, a squirrel once made by the two older Chernushkis for Ariadne when she was small, during the Russian Revolution. On these errands I usually spent the night at the Moulin du Coivre.

Once in a while our Russian friends managed to come in groups of two or three to our house or to the Moulin du Coivre. We drank tea, sang Russian songs, and had long talks about life in Russia. In these conversations it was an idealized Russia our friends were describing, as much for their own benefit as ours. It was as if they could not betray their country a second time by telling the truth about the life there. Perhaps they could not face the possibility that Russia would fail to become a better country after its ordeal.

Only Ivan Petrovich was careful to speak always with absolute truthfulness. My mother sensed this, and she loved him for it. I, too, thought of Ivan Petrovich as my favorite among our new friends. I trusted them all, even that show-off, Pedenko, who paid me outrageous court to the indignation of his more civilized comrades, but I trusted Ivan Petrovich the most. And he never said a word about how plentiful life had been in his small village before the war.

My father and Sasha formed another clan within our family. My father, who had never been in Russia under the Bolsheviks—he had fought in the civil war in the Caucasus against both the Reds and the Whites—was ready to believe that life in Russia had been improving. He had made up his mind that the great purges could never be repeated. Her sufferings would cleanse Russia. We were all absorbed by our Oléron adventures, yet my father still felt that "real life" was elsewhere, in distant Russia. Sasha believed him. We were going to go there, as soon as the war was over, to live among men like Leva and Ivan Petrovich. We would be happy: Russia was the country of *"grands ouvriers."*

One gray morning Misha Dudin burst into the Maison Ardeber. My mother and I were cleaning house—I remember that I was sweeping our dining room, noticing how very worn and ineffectual the old Ardeber broom had become. That June 6, at dawn, the Allies had started a landing operation in Normandy. American and British troops were gaining footholds on French soil. Misha was crying and laughing and embracing us. He danced a wild Ukrainian dance. It would now be only a matter of a few weeks before we would all be free—the Germans were in a state of panic.

By midafternoon, all of Saint-Denis knew of the landing. It was gigantic. The alarm which had seized the Germans was unmistakable: they were on full military alert.

That summer of 1944 was the first short summer of my life, a foretaste of things to be, an acceleration of time that has not relented since. The Russian soldiers were constantly coming up with new ideas for a military takeover of the island. Every night, we crossed rue du Port to Colonel Merle's house and listened to the news: the Allies were conquering France. The battles were often indecisive, the advance slow, but after the years of immobility in Western Europe, this movement filled us with a joy that was all the stronger for being controlled in public.

For many weeks we lived in a state of euphoria, which the

beauty of summer and our friendship with the Russians intensified. Paris was freed in August, and Rochefort, on the mainland only thirty or forty kilometers from Oléron as the crow flies, in September. We were on the eve of freedom. I remember riding to the Moulin du Coivre with the squirrel stuffed with documents tied to the bicycle rack, feeling no fear whatever, only a sense of importance.

My clearest recollection out of that time is an afternoon on the beach on a windy, overcast day toward the end of the summer. My father, Ivan Petrovich, Misha, and I had gone swimming. The tide was very high. Even on the sheltered beach near the jetty, the waves were formidable, but I no longer feared the surf. I had learned how to plunge into the biggest wave, to swim beyond it to where long swells lifted one up and down slowly, as if the ocean itself were breathing. Screeching sea gulls circled above our heads. The sky was darker than the sea, the breaking waves made glistening patterns as the water licked the yellow sand. I felt safe. The memory of that afternoon is one of the happiest out of those years.

Weeks went by, and our hopes for a prompt liberation were denied. After their initial wave of panic, the Germans were entering into a new role. Once they had been vacationers on the island; now, having turned it into a fortress, they would withstand an indefinite siege within it. Hitler had always taken a personal interest in the defenses of the Atlantic wall. He had looked into the minutest details of its construction: "The Führer highly disapproves of insufficiently protected openings in the bunkers. . . ."

Linked to Berlin through the radio and by air, the Germans were to stand steadfast on the Atlantic shore. Eventually a mighty counterattack would free them. This maneuver was already taking shape in the Ardennes in a grandiose, secret plan supervised by the Führer personally.

The Germans became stricter with the foreigners within their ranks. The Russians were sometimes detained in their batteries for weeks on end. As fall came with its long rains, they became increasingly dispirited. We saw them less often, with the exception of Misha and Ivan Petrovich; the peaceable temperament of these two, combined with the benevolence of their Austrian sergeant, left them relatively free to go about Saint-Denis. Leva, too, continued to come to the Moulin du Coivre in Saint-Pierre almost daily. Inaction plunged him into a state of quiet anger, which alarmed the Sossinskys. Yet, for the time being, the unequivocal orders from the mainland were to abstain from hostile acts against the Germans. It was as if we were aboard an abandoned vessel. With each day their inaction became more unnerving for the Russians—their chance to rehabilitate themselves in battle was slipping away.

What to us seemed like drifting was in part, at least, a calculated plan not to escalate warfare—the outcome of secret, unofficial talks between two adversary commanding officers, the German commander of La Rochelle, Admiral Shirlitz, and a French naval officer, Captain Meyer. Stories about bloodshed abounded; the fact that these men endeavored to save human lives at the height of the war engages the imagination. But we were not to learn of this until much later.

One day in November an enormous explosion resounded on the island. Along rue du Port there was a sound of broken glass like prolonged, high-pitched laughter. Within minutes, German cars were racing past our house with a screeching of tires. A truck full of soldiers roared in the direction of Saint-Pierre, followed by an excavator, which clambered ponderously through the village like a gigantic prehistoric animal, rumbling away on the road to Méray. My father, coming home from his fields, said that out in the open one could see a thick tower of black smoke rising from the middle of the island.

The next day, toward noon, my grandmother arrived at the Maison Ardeber. She was breathless, her eyes sparkled. Leva and his friend, the young Red Army engineer Dmitri, had blown up the island's main arsenal at La Perroche. Saint-Pierre was under tight surveillance—my grandmother had reached Saint-Denis along the chalky back roads meandering through the vineyards.

That morning Leva had come by the Moulin du Coivre for about five minutes. He was jubilant. He and his friend had acted on their own—and been successful. They had known that, had they asked for approval from the Resistance, they would once again have been forbidden to act. Nor had the other Russians on the island been told about the plot—they would be relatively safe from reprisals even if Leva and Dmitri were caught. The island's main arsenal was annihilated along with the dozen men guarding it. Dmitri, a twenty-year-old student of engineering, had made a fuse which had burned for more than five hours. All four Russians stationed in La Perroche—the two of them and two other, older men—had been at work on a far-away construction project at the time of the explosion.

The Russians throughout the island were interrogated by the gestapo, but the cause of the explosion at La Perroche was never discovered. The Germans brought in ammunition from La Rochelle and distributed it throughout their batteries—no new central arsenal was created on the island. The site of the explosion, two kilometers from the Sossinskys' house, looked like a great crater with fantastically shaped segments of concrete and twisted metal scattered all around it. The Germans were reluctant to come close to that crater studded with unexploded mines. They surrounded it instead with a flimsy fence of barbed wire marked with skull-and-crossbone signs. It was to stand untouched for years after.

The explosion had frightened the Germans. They no longer smiled as they went about Saint-Denis. One day they requisitioned all the islanders' bikes. Luckily, our old *clous* were not taken because of their sorry condition. By then, my father's was without tires. As a substitute, he had looped a heavy rope around the wheels.

Soon afterward the commandant ordered all radio receivers to be delivered to the German authorities. The inhabitants of Saint-Denis brought their beloved radios in their veneer cabinets to the Mairie, never to see them again. Those who did not give up their radios were threatened with martial law, but some, like Colonel Merle and Andrei Kalita, kept theirs anyway, burying them deeper into thick walls. To bring these out from their caches was a lengthy ritual which took place every evening behind barricaded windows and doors. As fall turned to winter, the Germans cut off entirely the civilians' electric current, but a member of the Saint-Denis Resistance group, Monsieur Foucaud, a displaced Parisian worker, knew how to manipulate the wires atop the appropriate electric pole, a risky procedure resorted to only by the few who had kept their radios.

All through Oléron's late fall, with its twilight colors and its endless evenings, we knew what was going on in the world through our friends' radios. In the Vosges Mountains, in Alsace, the Allies' sweep toward Germany was stopped. For us, too, life seemed arrested; it had the taste of sea mist, it smelled of dolphin oil, of mushrooms, of the pine cones burning in our fireplace. Our enameled Godin stove had collapsed with age, and the fireplace behind it was opened up. We used it for heating and lighting the dining room. We also did some of our cooking in it, roasting potatoes under the ashes.

After the evening news, Colonel Merle visited with us by the fireside. He told us about his youth before World War I. It was hard to read for long by a dolphin oil lamp, and lighthearted stories, those of the colonel, or my grandmother's about her student years in Odessa, sounded magical. Once there had been peace throughout Europe, perhaps peace would return one day and war be only a remembrance.

On December 13 my father finished one of his monthly, two-week-long work periods for the Germans. To celebrate his forthcoming two weeks of freedom, he went mushroom-gathering in the woods of Boyardville with Andrei Kalita. By dusk he came home with two big fishing baskets filled with that delectable mushroom, *Lactarius deliciosus*, which we especially appreciated because it is at its best preserved in salt, a year-round staple.

My father had returned to Saint-Denis alone that afternoon—on the way home, Kalita had stopped in La Brée. A peasant lived there whose red wine made with the deep blue grape Othello was famous on the island. Kalita wanted to taste his 1944 vintage. At the Maison Ardeber, we stayed up late sorting out the mushrooms in the faint light of the dolphin oil lamp.

That night my father was led away by five German soldiers with bayoneted rifles. When I came in from the salon where I slept he was gone, but the dining room was still filled with the smell of leather and of machine oil. I had not heard the banging at the kitchen door, nor the shouts. From outside, the soldiers had summoned my father; he was under arrest. As he was getting dressed, trying to cheer up my mother, he told her that just before waking, he had been dreaming that he was fixing the sole of his shoe—he was always repairing something in those years on Oléron. He had awakened when the banging of his hammer had become the banging of the Germans downstairs.

I looked out into the empty garden. I still recall the ghostly appearance of the yucca in the predawn darkness, its spikey leaves like sharp knives reaching to the sky—and the fear which filled us, my mother and me, and which we tried to repress. Sasha was brave throughout that day and the ones that followed. While my father was getting dressed, he had awakened. My father had kissed him and told him that he would be back soon.

A terrified Madame Kalita came by for a minute that morning, December 14. In addition to my father, four men in the village had been arrested—Andrei Kalita, Foucaud, Monsieur Dupeux, and Monsieur Guyonnet. Then the town crier made his rounds: no one was allowed to leave Saint-Denis without a permit from the Kommandantur. Women and children were to stay home; all the men in the village were to proceed immediately to the Mairie.

Within minutes, frightened men were walking by the Maison Ardeber in the direction of the Mairie while their wives, in tears, stood in the doorways. Then an abrupt silence descended on rue du Port. At exactly twelve o'clock three Germans, an officer and two soldiers, walked into our garden— the sound of their boots identified the Germans even before they could be seen. They were under orders to search the house. Only minutes before, my mother and I had buried a tin box stuffed with scraps of paper next to the "thinking wall." One of the documents concerned the parachuting of weapons to the Saint-Denis group. Two days before, at the request of Armagnac, my father and Colonel Merle had chosen a secluded field between La Brée and Saint-Denis for this purpose and had drawn a map of it that was to be delivered to Volodia.

The Germans stepped into our house weightily, their weapons clanging. Evidently they were looking for firearms and for radio equipment; they left no closet unexplored, no bed unturned. They looked in the stove, behind armoires, in cabinets. The search lasted a full three hours. Despite the chilly weather, Sasha and I took refuge in the garden. The Germans started with André's room, the one with the French doors opening into the garden. We heard a gasp as they were confronted with the pickled snake inside the desk.

When they were done with André's room, I settled there with a book, something lighthearted out of Madame Marquet's library. The snake that had startled the Germans had become a friendly presence. In the garden, Sasha was playing quietly. In his own corner there, he was building himself a cabin out of old planks. Once in a while he would come into the house, then go out again. I, too, went into the garden and climbed on the "thinking wall." I could overhear the men speaking to each other and a few words of German said by my mother in a gentle voice as the salon was searched—a lengthy task in view of its elaborate furnishings. I was thinking about my father—where had they taken him? There were no more trains in the direction of Germany. It all had to be like a folktale, terrifying perhaps but ending well. For the Germans had in effect been defeated. Hitler would not become the master of the universe.

In the garden I heard the officer say good-bye to my mother quite politely. Then they walked up to Monsieur Masson's house next door. Monsieur Masson, his face ashen, let them in through the door with the tarnished brass knocker in the shape of a beautiful hand.

My mother was exhausted. As we sat down to a meal of linden tea and cornmeal bread, she told me how she had just saved from destruction that beautiful armoire in my grandmother's room, the one to which even Mademoiselle Charles had no keys. "As they got to the salon and began searching, I remembered about the armoire," she said. "The Germans were opening everything in the house. How could we be so careless, keeping a locked wardrobe in our house? The officer wouldn't believe me when I said that I didn't have a key to the armoire. 'This is impossible. You have an armoire in your house and you cannot open it? Please bring me an appropriate tool, and *I'll* open it for you!'

"Sasha had just wandered in and I asked him to bring the axe from the kitchen, and he found it behind the stove and brought it. One of the soldiers took it and raised it, about to strike a blow. I said in German to the officer: 'Such a beautiful antique. Aren't you ashamed?' Nothing else. The officer made a movement and stopped the soldier, who put the axe down. The search was over. How lucky that we had time to bury the tin box! Not that they looked at papers carefully, but they certainly did empty out the little mahogany secretary in my room and Mother's desk downstairs."

Unknown to us, my mother had saved not only an Ardeber heirloom but also our lives. We were to learn after the war that the eighteenth-century armoire of carved fruitwood contained a veritable arsenal—Docteur Ardeber's hunting rifles and several hundred loaded cartridges. Saint Denis himself had been looking after us that day.

Clara's Return

By four o'clock that day, the town crier had once again made his rounds. Even sterner curfew hours were to go into effect, from 6:00 P.M. to 8:00 A.M. Then the men of the village who had been locked up in the Mairie were released. A sigh of relief went through the town as the men walked home in small groups. Soon everyone was out in the street again. On Oléron people had heard of Oradour, a whole village which had been massacred by the Germans the summer before. In quiet voices, in their elliptic Oléronais manner, they were exchanging impressions. Many had believed that they would be killed, like the men of Oradour.

After a while Vera Kalita and Bebka arrived at the Maison Ardeber. Although her house had not been searched, Vera Kalita, left alone without her husband, had been plunged into a state of terror. Now she was showering improbable advice on my mother, about how to manage our household in my father's absence, what to do with the rabbits and with our temperamental goat that lived in Monsieur Masson's garden. One of Vera Kalita's ideas was that she and my mother should call on the commandant of Saint-Denis and fall at his feet, confessing their husbands' underground activities and pleading for mercy.

When my mother, looking shocked, tried to divert Madame Kalita by asking her about the health of her rabbits, which had been stricken by an epidemic a few days before, our guest suggested that perhaps she and my mother should plead for their husbands' release, falling at the commandant's feet—but without a confession, not till accusations against them were put forth. The present commandant, Colonel Wohl, was such a decent man—why not take advantage of this before Armagnac was uncovered?

My mother kept her self-control, although she became quite pale. She suggested that I walk Madame Kalita home. Then I was to stop by Madame Marquet's and ask her to spend the night with Madame Kalita in her cottage. There was no telling what idea might enter her head, and Madame Marquet, despite her occasional intercourse with spirits, was a woman of good sense and of sound patriotic instincts.

When I returned to the Maison Ardeber in the December darkness, minutes before the curfew, I could not believe my eyes. The whole long day had to be an episode out of some menacing fairy tale. Clara Rittoni was standing in our dining room, warming herself by the fireplace, while my mother, looking anxious, was fixing supper. How lucky that our two visitors had not met! Vera Kalita would have lost her mind on the spot at the sight of Clara.

But Clara was not discussing the Kalitas now, nor my father's arrest. Rubbing her hands, she was telling my mother about her studies in the English language. A secret agent from the League of Nations, sent especially from Switzerland to Oléron, had contacted her in Saint-Trojan, to make sure that she would join it as soon as peace had returned to Europe. And then she had in her possession such fascinating documents! Clara was enigmatic, but the implication was that it was an explosive diary by one of the higher-placed participants of the July 20, 1944, abortive plot against Hitler's life, which had mysteriously been placed in her hands for safekeeping.

I went upstairs to read a bedtime story to Sasha, Chukovsky's Russian version of *Doctor Doolittle.* It muffled Clara's voice, which made me think of the early years of the war, when there seemed to be no hope for us, or for the world. At that moment it sounded sinister; was Clara like Poe's raven, which would *never* go from our life? Was she Vii's witch out of Gogol's terrifying tale, who never lets go of the young seminarist whom she possesses?

Unmindful of the curfew, Clara stayed on. When she finally left and we sat down to supper, my mother told me the several remarkable things that she had just heard, more remarkable even than the news of Clara's future job at the League of Nations.

First, Clara had just discovered that she had a serious heart ailment. She had resigned as the island's interpreter. The kindly Colonel Bourrade, Paul's godfather, had asked her to stay in his house. His daughters, Gigi and Roberte, who loved her like an older sister, would nurse her back to health. Her room was being readied, but she had wanted to come by while she still could, to give moral support to my mother. It broke her heart to abandon her mission in the service of the inhabitants of the island which she had carried on from Saint-Trojan, but it had to be if she were to live. In any case, the Germans themselves were about to fire her because they were aware of her pro-French sympathies.

Second, Clara had promised a laissez-passer, duly issued by the German Kommandantur, authorizing my mother to go the next day to Boyardville to visit my father. The document would be waiting for my mother at the Mairie in the morning; Clara's own bicycle would be there too, should my mother want to borrow it, since she could not ride my father's tireless *clou*. According to Clara, about three hundred men from all over the island had been taken that morning to Boyardville, to the deserted children's home in the pines known, ironically enough, as Maison Heureuse. It was to serve as a concentration camp until the prisoners' cases were individually examined.

"This wave of arrests is a preventive measure," Clara had said. "Colonel Wohl himself has told me so. They are so stupid, those Germans! They have seized many of their own sympathizers, such as that scoundrel, Kalita, while the leaders of the local Resistance, like Colonel Bourrade, are still free." This was on the whole reassuring—Clara apparently knew nothing about Armagnac.

Colonel Merle was splendid in the days that followed my father's arrest. He helped care for our goat, my father's exclusive charge until then, which had a fiendish disposition and a determination to upset the milking bucket whenever she had a chance. He assisted us with household tasks—he split the driftwood we used, along with pine cones, for the kitchen stove. He helped clean the rabbit cages. He also made decisions about the parachuting of weapons to Saint-Denis. Since my mother had a laissez-passer for Boyardville, on her way back she would make a stop at the Moulin du Coivre to deliver the parachuting map to Volodia—assuming that my uncle had not been arrested. Clara had said that she thought, on the basis of what she had overheard at the Kommandantur, that he had not.

In midmorning, on Clara's bicycle, my mother set forth for Boyardville. She found Maison Heureuse easily at the edge of the woods. Its stucco buildings, with their washed-out blue shutters and their abandoned playgrounds, were enclosed with a barbed-wire fence, at least five meters high. The gates were guarded by German soldiers with machine guns. Upon presentation of her laissez-passer, she was taken into the office of the commandant. Within minutes, led by an armed soldier, my father was brought into the commandant's office and allowed to embrace her.

Between questions about the children and the garden, my father was able to whisper in Russian that though several members of Armagnac had been seized, it did not appear that the Germans had any specific knowledge about the underground. The atmosphere among the Frenchmen was vehemently anti-German, with a lot of French cockiness. Oléron's leading citizens suspected of anti-German opinions had been taken, along with a few individuals without roots on the island, like my father and the Parisian, Foucaud.

In his normal voice, my father recounted that he had a berth next to Andrei Kalita—Kalita was a formidable snorer at night. In the daytime, he was a good comrade. My mother gathered that, through his arrest, Kalita felt that he had at last been recognized as an anti-Nazi. With dismay, she recalled Vera Kalita's behavior the day before, but she was unable to discuss it with my father. Speaking of Kalita and of his legendary appetite, my father was saying that it looked as if the prisoners might be well fed. The kitchen at Maison Heureuse would be run by the prisoners themselves: provisions were to be supplied by their families. Enough prosperous peasants, fishermen, and oystermen had been arrested to make this a promising prospect, even if the Germans were to levy a share of supplies. That morning, lavish baskets of fish from La Cotinière and fresh vegetables from Saint-Trojan had been brought into the camp.

Before they parted my mother conveyed to my father the fact that she was taking his and Colonel Merle's map to Volodia. She was going to spend the night at the Sossinskys'—Sasha and I would sleep at Vera Kalita's. I was to make sure that she did not rush off to Colonel Wohl.

As she was led out of Maison Heureuse by two German soldiers armed with machine guns, my mother's last vision of the camp was that of Monsieur Guyonnet, standing on one of the wooden balconies of Maison Heureuse. Monsieur Guyonnet was brushing energetically the black suit he wore at all times as a sign of his dignity as the director of the school of Saint-Denis. She waved to him, and he waved back.

It turned bitterly cold as my mother followed the road from Boyardville to Saint-Pierre. Her permit did not specifically allow a detour through Saint-Pierre, and she was afraid that she might be stopped by a German patrol. When she finally reached the Moulin she felt like Scarlett O'Hara returning to Tara, to the safety of home—only to be greeted there by new disasters. For though Volodia had not been arrested, the atmosphere at the Moulin du Coivre was tense as the family sat down to a supper of polenta with tomato sauce. Volodia, always so gay, was uncommunicative that evening. Ariadne had her small dry cough. Only my grandmother was herself, serving polenta to everyone with her customary solicitude. My mother could not understand what was upsetting the Sossinskys to such a degree. She had extracted the folded map from inside one of her rubber boots and given it to Volodia. My uncle had taken it distractedly. Only after Aliosha had gone to bed did she hear the news the family was trying to conceal from the small boy.

Four days before, on December 11, one of the Russians had fled from his battery near Saint-Pierre and taken refuge at the Moulin du Coivre. The Sossinskys had seen him only once before, and they had not liked him. A short, squarish man from central Russia, Rybov was a silent, unhappy man, and his comrades distrusted him. He was among the dozen Russians on the island not working for Réseau Armagnac. Its very existence had been kept from him, but Rybov had guessed that the Sossinskys were involved in anti-German activities.

Arriving at their house at sunset, Rybov had demanded that the Sossinskys hide him. The Germans were mean to him, meaner to him than to anyone else. Volodia, a Russian patriot, should help him escape to the mainland. My uncle pointed out that the Moulin du Coivre was under scrutiny by German patrols and that Rybov's presence there might cause the whole Sossinsky family to be shot. Rybov was unmoved. He refused to return to his battery.

When Volodia ordered the intruder out of his house, Rybov became angry. Should he be sent back to his German unit, he would be beaten—and he could not stand physical violence. "If the Germans as much as touch me, I will tell them—everything! Everything I know, and everything I do not know, about you and the other Russians on the island!" Volodia had no alternative but to allow the fugitive to settle in the old mill next to the house, where he slept on the ground wrapped in a blanket. The next day Volodia was able to persuade him to come to the distillery. There he found him a hiding place at the bottom of an enormous copper caldron that had been used for the making of cognac.

Now abandoned, this caldron stood in a remote spot at the back of the distillery. Volodia brought food and water to Rybov every night while the distillery was empty save for the old watchman who lived at the other end of the building. Climbing a ladder at the side of the vat, Volodia dropped the supplies to Rybov inside. Rybov was complaining and threatening, accusing my uncle of plotting to deliver him to the Germans: clearly, he was mentally unstable.

In the days that followed, my mother and I spent a great deal of time with Vera Kalita, who was as insistent as ever in getting my mother to see Colonel Wohl. We worried about my father in his camp and about the fugitive at the bottom of the caldron in Saint-Pierre. One day, through the Mairie, I obtained a laissez-passer to visit my father. However, when I reached Boyardville on his old bicycle, the Germans would not let me in: visitors were now forbidden at Maison Heureuse. I remember my intense disappointment and the malevolent aspect of what must once have been a happy summer home for children. The barbed-wire fences with machine gun nests here and there made it look like a real concentration camp.

Somehow informed of my presence at the gates of the camp—someone from Saint-Denis must have seen me from the distance—my father suddenly appeared at the barbed-wire fence as I bicycled alongside it on my way out of the woods. He looked in good health, although his new beard made him look much older. We had time to exchange a few sentences before a German soldier, without any particular show of anger, came after him and led him away. Everything was well with him, my father had time to say, despite the fact that a gestapo unit, now permanently assigned to Maison Heureuse, was conducting a detailed investigation of each prisoner. To his knowledge, nothing about Réseau Armagnac had been uncovered so far. I had time only to whisper that, because of the arrests, the parachuting of weapons to the Saint-Denis unit had been postponed. Then I bicycled straight to Saint-Pierre.

At the Moulin du Coivre, the atmosphere was strained. Ariadne still was coughing nervously although she contained her feelings, as always. My grandmother, on the other hand, as befitted an old revolutionary, was calm, cheering everyone up. We spent the afternoon reading aloud Lermontov's poem about medieval Georgia, "The Demon." Aliosha listened too, and this diverted us until Volodia came home from the distillery. At the bottom of the vat, Rybov was still carrying on in an irrational, aggressive manner. Now he was accusing Volodia of wanting to poison him. Leva had dropped by the distillery under the guise of buying a bottle of cognac. He had said that the other Russians on the island were afraid of the defector, that the German military police were looking for him all over the island.

Volodia had intended to kill Rybov that very morning—in his briefcase he had taken an axe—but he had been incapable of striking a half-demented man in cold blood. Instead he would ask the Armagnac unit from Le Château for help.

Volodia requested that I bicycle to Le Château early the next morning. A skinny fourteen-year-old on an ancient bicycle would attract little attention in the middle of the day. He was right—I had no difficulty delivering an oral message from Volodia to the wife of a fisherman who lived near the market square. That morning, Le Château's lovely Renaissance square was teeming with Germans. The castle above it, built on the site where Eleanor of Aquitaine had proclaimed the first maritime code in history—*les Rôles d'Oléron*—was surrounded with artillery pieces under camouflage netting. Le Château looked like a fortress readying itself for an attack.

The woman to whom I spoke had an expressionless face. She was in black—even her kissnot was black. She said nothing as I recited a coded message requesting that "Raoul come to see Joseph immediately." As I bicycled back to Saint-Denis, I tried to remember the lines out of the *Rôles d'Oléron* which I had read in a history book from the Lutins' library. They sounded like poetry, these laws from the twelfth century, more sensible than the twentieth:

> A vessel is in the harbor, awaiting its freight and the weather. The hour of sailing has come; the Master must consult his companions: "Gentlemen, does the weather suit you? Should we sail?" Some will say: "The weather is not good; it has not yet settled. We must let the weather settle!" Others will say: "The weather is beautiful and good." The Master will take the opinion of the greater number of his companions. . . .

Vera Kalita revived her plan to intercede with the Germans for the release of her husband: in my absence she had had a confrontation with my mother. Stopping by on her way back from gathering periwinkles for her ducks, she insisted once again that my mother's duty to her children and husband was to try to get my father out of the Germans' hands. At Colonel Wohl's suggestion, she had made an appointment to see the commandant of Boyardville—"Together with Frau Andreyev, the mother in distress of two small children." They would be received by the commandant on the very next day. When my mother once again declined, Vera Kalita had rushed out of the house, a pathetic figure with her dripping basket of seashells and her small dog on a leash.

I decided to go see her at once, before the curfew. Perhaps reassuring news of her husband would persuade her to give up her project. However, Vera Kalita was intractable. She looked worn out: what with caring for the geese, the ducks, and the rabbits, she was overwhelmed with work. Much as I disapproved of her readiness to deal with the Germans, I could understand her desire to have the master of the house back. She asked me to come by the next day to show her the way to Boyardville, where she had never been.

"You cannot go, this is a ruse," my mother said firmly when I came home. "As she leaves on her dishonorable expedition, Vera Kalita wants to be seen in the company of a member of our family, to give herself some respectability—nothing ever escapes the Oléronais' watchful eye."

We did not see Vera Kalita for several days after that. We became absorbed by the Rybov drama. Misha Dudin and Ivan Petrovich told us that the other Russians throughout the island were restive—Rybov's disappearance had resulted in a stiffening of military discipline. From them, we learned that Leva had offered to shoot Rybov, but my uncle had ruled this out as too dangerous.

The following week, without a laissez-passer, my intrepid grandmother came again to the Maison Ardeber by way of back roads. She wanted to tell us about the improbable dénouement of the Rybov adventure. Volodia had persuaded "Raoul" from Armagnac to organize the transfer of the fugitive to the mainland. One day at noon, a young fisherman from Le Château, still almost an adolescent, had arrived at the distillery bringing a second bicycle along with his own.

While the employees of the distillery were out to lunch, Rybov was extracted from his hiding place, fed, and given a shot of cognac. He was put on one of the two bicycles: he was to ride some distance behind the young man, who would lead him to an isolated spot along the coast. There he was to be picked up by a fisherman in a flatboat, the kind the Germans tolerated around the oyster beds of Le Château. This boat would head for the mainland after dark.

As Rybov climbed on his bike he had seemed in good enough spirits and fairly steady on his legs, despite his ten-day incarceration in the caldron. In his German uniform, he was to bicycle behind the fisherman as if he did not know him. It was unlikely that the two would meet a German patrol along the dirt roads running between abandoned salt beds that they were to follow, but were this to happen, the Frenchman would divert the Germans' attention by accosting them, and feigning drunkenness. This would give Rybov a chance to disappear among the thick tamarisk bushes growing along the salt marshes. The day was misty yet completely calm—the chances for the plan to work were excellent.

But a couple of hours later the young fisherman was back at the distillery—alone. Rybov had disappeared in the fog. The two had proceeded peacefully along the salt beds, or so the fisherman thought, but at a certain moment, as he had glanced backward, he no longer could see the Russian. He had stopped and waited, then he had gone back some distance, but Rybov was not to be seen anywhere. Like the legendary Russian warlock of the swamps, he had vanished in the fog. The young fisherman found his abandoned bicycle in the bushes not far from where he had last seen him.

Since neither the Sossinskys nor any of our Russian friends were touched by the Germans in the days that followed, we assumed that Rybov had not been caught—not yet. We took the return home of Andrei Kalita shortly before Christmas as a good omen. Had Rybov talked about Réseau Armagnac as he had threatened to do, Kalita might not have been released.

At first Kalita was angry with his wife for having him freed on special orders from the commandant of Boyardville. He had been enjoying his predicament—I think that he did not mind being away from Vera Kalita, from the dog, the geese, the ducks, and the rabbits. Above all, he had at last been given a chance to suffer in the name of Russia. He had thrived in the atmosphere of comradeship at the Maison Heureuse. Along with a couple of affluent greengrocers and oystermen from the southern part of the island, he had been one of the kings of Maison Heureuse—a great chef, he had a hand in the running of the kitchen. But he soon came to terms again with freedom in Saint-Denis. He worked on Armagnac business with Colonel Merle and fattened his geese and ducks for the New Year.

However, on the evening of Kalita's return from Boyardville, he was still under the spell of the shared dangers of the Maison Heureuse. He had stopped by our house first to give us news of my father, and to vent his bitterness before confronting his overzealous spouse. Our reunion was tumultuous—there were hugs, good wishes, promises to help us with our household, and a ceremonious toast drunk with the best cognac. My mother sent Sasha across the street to fetch Colonel Merle. Kalita briefed the colonel about the excellent morale of Armagnac behind bars.

Having obtained a safe conduct to Saint-Pierre, we spent Christmas there. The fears provoked by Rybov's disappearance had subsided, and, despite my father's absence, the atmosphere at the Moulin du Coivre was joyful: this would be our last Christmas under the Germans. Sasha and Aliosha were happy to be together again. Since there are no firs on Oléron, the Sossinskys had set up a young pine as a Christmas tree. And Leva was able to come by for a glass of mulled wine on Christmas Day.

That winter, the weather was fiendish, as it had been in 1940 and again in 1943, at the time of Stalingrad, as if the elements wanted once again to assert their powers over us. Sea storms succeeded one another, then the temperature dropped sharply. By the time we walked back to Saint-Denis just before the New Year, the pump in our garden was frozen. In the dark, Colonel Merle helped my mother revive it with hot ashes. At the last minute, its machinery was saved, and water flowed again in our kitchen.

For New Year's Eve, to greet 1945, we were invited to the Kalitas for duck stew, a specialty of Andrei Kalita's. The Sossinskys stayed in Saint-Pierre because of Armagnac's responsibilities, but my grandmother, who thrived on festivities, came to Saint-Denis despite the fierce cold.

On the night before the party, in spite of our efforts to dissuade him, Colonel Merle—who had also been asked to the Kalitas—went fishing with a lantern. This was extremely foolhardy, but he was undetected and came home with three large mullets. He gave one to us and took two to Madame

Kalita: the colonel could not go empty-handed to the Kalitas, where he had not been before. For a long time he had considered them disreputable, but now Kalita's wholehearted involvement with Armagnac had made it possible for him to accept their invitation.

We had a real party on New Year's Eve. Apprehension about my father never left us, yet we had had a note from him that day through a French electrician who worked in Maison Heureuse. My father wished us a happy New Year. The morale in the camp continued to be good. And Misha Dudin was able to come to the Kalitas' party that night. This was my first grown-up New Year's Eve.

We all fitted around the Kalitas' dining table, which was elegantly set: Vera Kalita had borrowed Madame Marquet's silverware and her high-stemmed Venetian wine glasses. Sasha's eyes shone as he sipped a little wine out of a tall gilded glass—he liked to be treated as a grown-up. We had a bottle of old Bordeaux brought by Colonel Merle; it smelled like summer on Oléron. The colonel's mullets, poached in white wine, were delicious. I barely noticed that the duck stew Andrei Kalita served seemed mostly made of duck's necks. Indeed, how many ducks had to be slaughtered to produce so many necks? It was a mystery, linked no doubt to the Kalitas' perennial fear of starvation.

We made our way home by way of Clara's lane, dashing in the dark between German patrols. The colonel had a nightcap by our fire. He had a mischievous smile on his bulldog face—now he looked like the Cheshire cat. He said nothing for a while, then he could no longer contain himself. "It was swan, of course! It was swan that Monsieur Kalita served us in that stew," he exclaimed. "What other animal possesses a neck long enough to feed all of us? 1945 will be the year of the swan—a winged year!"

Following the New Year, a new rumor began circulating in Saint-Denis: all the civilians not useful to the Germans would be evacuated from Oléron. This alarmed us—would we find ourselves completely cut off from my father? My mother decided to check this rumor with Clara at the Bourrades.

She found Clara looking well. Roberte and Gigi were nursing her with devotion, making her medicinal tea and plumping her pillows. Though she had been bedridden for nearly a month, Clara had remained in touch with the Kommandantur. Indeed, all those not indispensable to the economic survival of the German troops on Oléron were about to be sent into Free France. Clara had no notion of what might happen to the men in Boyardville. Their relatives would certainly be evacuated; another category of people, the notables of the island, like the Bourrades and herself, might have the option to leave. If this were true, Clara would of course go to Free France. After her recovery, a new life would be waiting for her at the League of Nations.

Unknown even to Clara, this evacuation plan reflected the secret negotiations that had been conducted since September between the French and German high commands. The surprisingly decent treatment of the prisoners in Maison Heureuse was one of the benefits of these negotiations. Despite the Free French high command's anxiety to prove itself through military deeds—General de Gaulle wanted France one day to participate in armistice talks—and the "scorched earth" policy Hitler was to proclaim soon afterward, Admiral Schirlitz and Captain Meyer had, on their own, reached a gentlemen's agreement not to escalate the fighting and to treat civilians and prisoners humanely.

Two days after my mother's visit to Clara, the town crier went from corner to corner, beating his drum. The inhabitants of the village were summoned to the Mairie to acquaint themselves with a list of those families who were to leave the island three days later. The Germans were ready to allow certain other persons to depart, as long as their presence was not indispensable to the economy of the island; peasants could not leave. Since our name began with *A*, we were first on a list of about ten families.

The Kalitas, Madame Guyonnet, Colonel Merle, Madame Dupeux, and the Foucaud family were among those from Saint-Denis who were to leave. That afternoon we heard that Clara and the Bourrades had decided to leave also. Then we learned through our Russian friends that the Sossinskys and my grandmother were being evacuated. My mother and I had three days to liquidate our household and try to raise some money— we had almost none. The colonel could not help us much—he, too, had a large house to put into order before leaving. He was desolate to see his Resistance activity come to an end, and his spirits were low. We tried to cheer him up: at least he had a place to go to—Châteaubriant on the mainland, where his family lived.

As for the Kalitas' establishment, ever so much bigger than ours or the colonel's, it was swept by madness. We had been told to take along enough food to last us several days and this alarmed the Kalitas—famine would be waiting on the mainland. The days allocated for packing witnessed a grandiose slaughtering of geese, ducks, chickens, and rabbits, and their transformation into various kinds of pâtés. It was a scene of carnage that lasted day and night until the very moment of departure: of the

Kalitas' animal kingdom, only Bebka was spared. Even Madame Marquet was overwhelmed despite her French lack of sentimentality and her respect for gastronomic values. "I begin to pity those poor beasts: it is not a good omen, all this blood," she said when she came to say good-bye to us.

I have a blurred recollection of our last days on Oléron. I do not think my mother and I ever worked so hard in our lives. Sasha was good-humored and helpful—we kept telling him that we were getting ready to join Papa. A rumor had it that some of the men from Maison Heureuse might leave with their families. We did not quite dare to believe it, but we packed my father's clothes in any case. We sewed some sacks out of old Ardeber curtains in which to more easily carry our belongings on our shoulders. These sacks were made of very old blue toile de Jouy printed with shepherds and frolicking goats. They looked like the luggage of fleeing émigrés in the French Revolution; perhaps they were symbolic, a reminder of how pastoral our life on Oléron had been.

Staying up until three or four o'clock in the morning, we worked and worked and my mother kept our spirits up by reciting poems she knew by heart: Pushkin, Pasternak, the most optimistic of all poets, and her favorite, Mandelstam. She recited that poem which she had read aloud in Vert-Bois many years before:

> Take for joy my wild present
> The plain dry necklace
> Of bees which died turning honey to sun.

Now our memories full of sunshine were tiny dead bees. We were leaving the island and our house, which would never be ours again. We had not discovered its secret, nor found the treasure buried somewhere within it. The belongings we were not taking with us, the books and clothing and toys, we stacked in the salon to be picked up in the future, if Saint-Denis and ourselves survived our liberation.

In the daytime, a flow of friends and neighbors came to say good-bye, to ask whether they could help, to bring small presents. The cobbler's wife bought our goat for 3,000 francs, an undreamed-of sum of money, which solved our financial problem. Perhaps she wanted to help? We did not know her very well. We gave our rabbits to Madame Marquet and to Madame Braud across the street. We sent a beautiful gray one as a present to the Austrian sergeant in Misha's battery. He had asked for one long ago, but we had done nothing about it at the time.

It was hardest of all to part with the Russians who were to remain inside the Atlantic wall in their German uniforms, "which burned them like clothes of fire." They were losing their direct connection with the French Resistance. Not that it would abandon them, the Russians were too useful for that, but the lack of a common language between them would make contacts difficult. Misha and Ivan Petrovich came to say goodbye to us on the eve of our departure, having sneaked out of their battery late at night. We gave them some tokens of our love, some Russian books, a few snapshots. I remember Ivan Petrovich crying, and Misha calling from the darkness of rue du Port, after my mother and I had walked him and his friend to our garden gate: "I love you as much as my own family! In fact, I love you *more*!" And that was the end of our friendship with the Russians from Russia. I was not to meet such Russians again until I went to Moscow in 1960.

Early that day, Leva had come by on bicycle. He was in a

terrible hurry and had only time to embrace us and to report that the Sossinskys and Olga Elyseevna had left that day, that the Moulin du Coivre now stood empty. And that rumor had it that Rybov had just been found by the Germans in the woods of Boyardville, half-dead from exposure. Evidently he had said nothing so far about Armagnac despite the rough treatment to which he was being subjected. Leva kept repeating as he hugged us: "You'll be able to leave before Rybov says anything to the Germans. You'll be able to leave, I feel it in my heart!"

Late in the morning on the following day, January 15, a bus arrived at Place de la Mairie. We had been waiting there in the icy wind for a long time, sitting on our luggage—about thirty of us, future refugees. I kept thinking about the Alsatians taken away by the Germans in 1940—where were they now? Sasha played quietly with the Foucauds' baby; he was always very good with small children. Vera Kalita sat by my mother, clutching her arm.

As we boarded the bus—Madame Guyonnet, Madame Dupeux, the colonel, the Foucauds, the blacksmith Coulon, the Kalitas with their immense baggage and a barking Bebka—I realized that neither the Bourrades nor Clara was there. So they had decided to stay behind after all. Fate was ridding us of Clara at the last minute. I remember that my heart was pounding as the bus puffed out of town—"No more Clara, no more Clara."

A World Free of Germans

The ride in that bus through the wintry Oléron landscape of bare, dark brown vineyards seemed endless. I could now think only of my father: might he perhaps be taken to that fortress on Ile de Ré, which was said to be a dungeon like Château d'If, where the Count of Monte Cristo had been imprisoned? As the bus finally reached the harbor of Boyardville, I saw a group of men in civilian clothing standing by the water's edge, guarded by a detachment of German soldiers. Among them was a man sitting in a wheelbarrow, like an oversized baby in a carriage.

A ferryboat was tied alongside the ancient stone quay, dwarfing it. The port of Boyardville, built by the great Vauban, dates back to the seventeenth century, and it looks formidable and toylike at the same time. In another second or two, I realized that the man in the wheelbarrow, who now was waving madly in the direction of the bus, was my father. In the crowd I recognized Monsieur Guyonnet, looking impeccable in his black suit; Monsieur Dupeux, who had not lost an ounce of weight; Monsieur Foucaud, with his Parisian's casquette pulled over one eye. The men on the quay looked radiant, even my father looked radiant as he sat up awkwardly in the wheelbarrow. What was the matter with him? This bizarre posture seemed but a continuation of all that was eerie in our adventures of the last weeks.

We were getting out of the bus, my father was hugging us. He had sprained his ankle when the other night's rain had frozen around Maison Heureuse. He had been carrying two buckets of soup—the soup had *not* spilled as he had fallen on the ice, but he had hurt himself. There were more hugs and a scramble for luggage, as the German soldiers hurried people onto the ferry. Minutes later, another bus bringing more refugees arrived, and then another. They were coming from other villages on the island. Families were reunited in bursts of confusion and joy. My father said that, unfortunately, not everyone from Maison Heureuse was being evacuated. At least thirty men were being sent on to the fortress on Ile de Ré.

We boarded the ferry at once. The afternoon was stormy. Andrei Kalita and the colonel helped my father aboard. Sasha led Bebka, barking and pulling on her leash, along a narrow, very steep gangplank. There was great urgency among the crew of French sailors in berets and rubber boots who were getting ready to sail. It was said that there had been a British submarine sighted nearby. People looked frightened.

We stood on deck for a last look at our island—at the low yellow beachline edged with black seaweed, the toylike bastions, the salt marshes with their sharp smell. The tide was rising. We saw the immense sky of Oléron that dwarfs the land. Suddenly, as the gangplank was about to be pulled up, a

ISLAND IN TIME

German ambulance drew up to the quay, followed by a black limousine. One by one, Colonel Bourrade, Madame Bourrade, Paul Rittoni, and finally Gigi and Roberte got out of the ambulance. The three Bourrade ladies were wearing French Red Cross uniforms with the white veil and the navy blue cap embroidered with a red cross. Then a stretcher was slowly pulled out of the ambulance by two German soldiers. On it lay Clara.

She was wrapped to her chin in a khaki blanket, her blond hair spilling over the pillow supporting her head. Her eyes were closed, she wore no makeup. Gently, she was carried aboard by the two Germans. Paul and the Bourrades followed. All were ushered into the captain's quarters somewhere in the center of the ship, disappearing from sight. In the meantime, several German soldiers were unloading the black limousine, carrying luggage up the gangplank. There was far more here than could be carried by hand by the Bourrades and the Rittonis—three steamer trunks and about twenty suitcases. Each was painted with a big red cross. I realized then that I had never believed Clara would fade out of our lives. Once again I was both repelled and fascinated.

About halfway to La Rochelle, the wind picked up and the sea became rough. It was said among the passengers that this was a good thing, that a submarine was less likely to attack us in stormy waters. The tiny ferry rocked violently. Suddenly, Paul came up on deck. He was green—he had just been seasick. He walked up to us, leaning against the railing between my father and my mother. He said to no one in particular: "My mother is not very sick. Soon she will be working in Geneva. The war will be over and we will be friends again, as we were before the Germans arrived, won't we? I like you, Vadim, and I like

André. I wonder how he is doing in Niort." My mother said something soothing about forgetting old quarrels. Soon all of us children would be going to school and leading normal children's lives. Indeed, my mother was right; I thought of our Russian friends, of Misha Dudin's laughing green eyes. Soon, Clara would only be a memory. We would live in Le Plessis and she in Geneva, and we would never see her again. Instead, the Russians from Russia would come for long visits with us.

Paul stood with us for a long time as the boat neared La Rochelle. We were greeted by the harbor's asymmetrical watch towers, which looked like two dark blue mountains. It was night when we docked, but there were no lights along the harbor. We could only make out the massive towers and hear the whistling of the wind and the loud splashing of the sea. A brazier was brought out; it cast spidery shadows as we came off the boat. There were billowing masses of barbed wire all along the quay. Young women in the khaki uniforms of the Pétainist welfare corps passed us mugs of hot, watery cocoa. Once again, Bebka was barking madly. In the crowd I lost sight of Paul and of the Bourrades with Clara.

The Saint-Denis contingent of refugees was now gathered in one spot on the quay. Someone said not to worry about the luggage, that it was safe to leave it behind. We started to walk in total darkness—my father was limping, supported in turn by Andrei Kalita and Colonel Merle. My mother held Sasha's hand on one side and mine on the other. We followed black tortuous streets between buildings which seemed to reach to the sky. We came at last to a monumental wooden door—Monsieur Guyonnet, who had lived in La Rochelle, said that this was the Hôtel-Dieu, the ancient city hospital.

We walked inside and up a wide stone staircase and along a

corridor. A nun from the order of Saint Vincent, wearing the spreading winged cap of that order, led us to a hall with a high Gothic ceiling and thirty or forty iron beds along its walls. This hall was dimly lit by two small electric bulbs. There was an enormous wooden crucifix at the far end of the room, where some beds were occupied by sleeping patients. Nuns in their white-winged caps appeared, showing us our beds—the men's on one side and the women's on the other. A warm meal was to be brought to us. The nuns moved about silently, speaking only in whispers. Their caps cast huge shadows on the walls. A sense of bliss descended upon us: we were safe, we had been reunited.

All of us from Saint-Denis slept soundly that night in the whiteness of hospital sheets—only Andrei Kalita's legendary snoring broke the silence. Before that Vera Kalita fretted because Bebka had not been allowed upstairs and had to spend the night instead in the kitchen of the Hôtel-Dieu. Had she been properly fed? Nonetheless, we were all happy. Colonel Merle had emerged from his depression, he was telling us about life in Châteaubriant: "Provincial but pleasant; my good wife is an excellent cook. What I shall miss there are the tides, the fishing." And he, Guyonnet, Kalita, and my father spoke for a long time in low voices about the way to contact Réseau Armagnac in Free France. How to make the French Resistance understand that our Russian friends were ready to fight the Germans from within the fortress Oléron?

Partly destroyed by bombardments, its glass roof gone, the railroad station in La Rochelle had been cleared and seemed to function normally that morning. I was dazed; I had not seen a train in six years, nor smelled the unique odor of a railroad station. Inside, in the area once sheltered by the glass ceiling, German soldiers were moving about.

The railroad platform was jammed with refugees. Ignoring each other, the contingent from Saint-Denis and the Rittoni-Bourrade group stood side by side, the ladies in navy blue Red Cross uniforms surrounding Clara on her stretcher. With loud exclamations, men came up to my father, who now had a walking stick to lean on, a broomstick given to him at the Hôtel-Dieu. These were my father's companions from the camp at Boyardville. There were bear hugs, slaps on the back, jokes, and from time to time, a sidelong glance in the direction of the Bourrades.

After a long wait a train made up of about fifteen passenger cars pulled alongside the platform. Impassive German officers verified the identity of each person climbing aboard. They examined attentively identity cards and safe conducts delivered by the Kommandantur, yet they never looked anyone in the face while we stood in line. Bebka was barking. Sasha picked her up while the Kalitas hauled up their weighty bags and baskets filled with jars of pâté and other culinary treasures. Then Clara was lifted on her stretcher and carefully carried into the train by two German soldiers. She was taken into a compartment having a huge red cross painted on the outside. The Bourrades and Paul followed her. The windowshade of the compartment was then promptly pulled down.

The train started moving. We looked at the disappearing Germans on the railway platform of La Rochelle. We were off to a world free of Germans.

We were off to a world free of Germans, yet we had no idea of where we were going. Even Andrei Kalita had been unable to find out our destination from the Germans on the quay. We took turns sitting in the window seats of our compartment. The train, which clanged along sedately, was well heated; everyone aboard had a seat. In our compartment, in addition to the four of us, sat Colonel Merle and the Guyonnets. The Kalitas had settled in the next compartment with the Dupeux. Clara and her party were in another car ahead of us. Whenever the train followed a leftward curve, one could see their compartment, its windowshade pulled up, the large red cross painted on the outside. I still despised Clara but not nearly as intensely as I had when the Germans were conquering the world. Now that they were losing the war, she was losing her power over our family. My mother was right. We, the young people, had to consider the best way to catch up with our studies, which languages to choose at the lycée, whether to take Latin or mathematics. I had not gone to school for almost four years.

Then I thought about Misha Dudin and Ivan Petrovich in their bunker in La Morelière above the ocean. And about poor Rybov. Had he been beaten by the Germans after they found him? How did he survive in the woods of Boyardville for more than ten days? It had been cold, there could have been no berries to eat, no mushrooms. Had he talked about Armagnac? He might be dangerous to the Russians on the island if he had. But perhaps he was not the coward the others said he was.

I thought about Clara again. Who would carry her on her stretcher at the other end of the journey, into that just world we were about to enter, where there would be no gentlemanly Germans? Might British or American soldiers do it? Or the FFIs? The FFIs, the Forces Françaises de l'Intérieur, were said to be very rough. Could Colonel Bourrade and Paul manage the stretcher by themselves? Or perhaps Clara would get up and walk, like the witch in Gogol's story "Vii," who arises from her coffin in the ancient wooden church? If only she would rise and fly away and disappear forever. . . .

I was awakened from my daydreaming by a jolt. The train had stopped in a landscape of meadows bordered with willow trees trimmed to look like orange kitchen mops. Cows grazed in the distance. Monsieur Guyonnet said that we were in the middle of the Marais Charentais. Only a couple of hundred years before, the sea had covered that area, then it had filled up, forming a lowland of grazing meadows that had produced the famous "Beurre des Charentes" before the war. A few minutes passed and the train pulled into the tiny station at Aigrefeuille. On the miniature railroad platform there were men who had to be Free French soldiers. They wore nondescript clothing, a mixture of worn khaki uniforms and civilian clothes.

Someone said that this was the border zone between German-held territory and Free France. There was no checking of passports in Aigrefeuille, only a brief exchange between a stiff, middle-aged German officer with a bony, hard face who had gotten off the train and the Frenchmen, who all wore navy blue berets and armbands painted with de Gaulle's emblem, the cross of Lorraine. To see that sign openly displayed was breathtaking—everyone in our compartment took turns leaning out of the window. Colonel Merle and Monsieur Guyonnet fell into each other's arms. Madame Guyonnet burst into tears—my mother held her hand. The train started again and accelerated, rushing us into Free France. Monsieur Guyonnet said that we were going north: "On this line, the next station has to be Surgère," he said. "Then comes Niort. You just might be spending the night at your Aunt Natasha's."

In another hour—we had had a picnic punctuated by friendly visiting from one compartment to another—the train pulled into a station called Surgère. By then I was thinking about Julien—where was he at that moment? was he alive?—and about Ronsard. Julien had once said that Ronsard's poem: *Quand vous serez bien vieille, assise à la chandelle* . . . which I particularly liked, hoping secretly that he would celebrate me someday in that manner, was addressed to a lady named Hélène de Surgère. Had Hélène been beautiful? Was her castle nearby, somewhere behind the harlequin-patterned fencing of the railroad station?

There were no Germans in Surgère—the last German in uniform I was ever to see had been that officer in Aigrefeuille, whose stern bony face I still remember today. It was here in Surgère that our train would be checked by Free French authorities. Madame Kalita, in a state of extreme nervousness, came into our compartment and sat next to my mother. Trying to be inconspicuous, she gave her a package of photographs tied with a ribbon. My mother put it at once in her purse. These were the pictures of Vera Kalita's sons in German uniforms that my mother had promised to take across the border for her.

Now FFI soldiers were boarding the train and checking the passengers' identities. They were friendly and very businesslike. Colonel Merle told one of them that he wanted to make a report about the activities of Réseau Armagnac on the island of Oléron. At once the man summoned an officer: such a report should be given to the FFI headquarters in Niort, our next stop. He was a dark-haired man about thirty years old, with a marked southern accent. "I am myself from the province of Armagnac," he said. "I know about Réseau Armagnac—they are now gathering nearby, in the town of Cognac."

The officer said that Niort might be our final destination. "But then the train could be rerouted south," he added. "There is an overflow of refugees in the region. In the last two days trains from Oléron, Ré, and Royan have been headed there one after another. Thousands of people. Yes, you might be taken elsewhere, as far as Périgueusc or even Agen, my hometown." He offered Gauloises to the men in our compartment. *"Vive la France! Vive l'Armagnac!"* he called out as he left, having shaken hands with my father, Monsieur Guyonnet, and Colonel Merle.

The train remained for a long time in Surgère, where the air itself was different because there were no Germans. We were in a new world, we were free. I looked out the window eagerly. The railway platform curved leftward. Whenever I leaned out of the window, I could see the compartment marked with the large red cross.

I noticed that Colonel Bourrade had gotten out of the train. He was a small man with a scrubby moustache across his narrow frowning face. On the platform he talked for a long time with two FFI officers—his manner was imperious. From the window it looked as if the three men were on stage, acting out a play. Following Colonel Bourrade, the officers climbed into the train and came out again. I noticed that Clara's shade was again pulled down. FFIs were walking along the corridor of our car, calling out: *"Vive la France! Bon voyage! Prochain arrêt, Niort!"* and waving good-bye.

Then, as the train seemed about to depart, and after its whistle had already sounded, three FFI men armed with pistols suddenly made their way to the compartment beyond us. Vera and Andrei Kalita, who was carrying Bebka, were being led out, past the glass partition of our compartment. Now they were standing below us on the platform looking terrified, Bebka barking furiously.

Forgetting his ankle, my father dashed onto the quay, followed by Monsieur Guyonnet and Colonel Merle. Bumping into the FFI soldiers who were taking out the Kalitas' luggage, they made their way toward the Kalitas and the men surrounding them. A confrontation that looked highly theatrical took place within sight of our compartment window. We could hear Colonel Merle shouting "Treason!" and see him waving his arms. The FFIs remained amicable and restrained. Ignoring him, they kept showing a paper to my father and Guyonnet.

The train gave a jerk. The FFIs pushed the three men—but not the Kalitas—toward the train: they had just time to climb aboard. We were leaving. Leaning out of the window, my mother and I had a last vision of the Kalitas in the middle of the platform, their baggage scattered around them. Madame Kalita waved feebly in our direction. Bebka barked.

When my father and his two friends reached our compartment, they were angry and out of breath. Clara had denounced Kalita and his wife to the French authorities as dangerous collaborators, using as proof that exemption from work on the Atlantic wall that she had translated into French for the Mairie eighteen months before.

My father was pale and sat very still in his corner. Madame Guyonnet, who did not particularly like the Kalitas—she was an incarnation of French old-fashioned working-class propriety—once again had burst into tears. Refugees from other parts of the island came up to our compartment to ask for details, to vent their indignation against "La Tarpette." The happiness that had carried us along since the night before vanished. We had left the Germans behind, but evil was still with us. I kept thinking about that witch in Gogol's story standing in her coffin—had Clara gotten up from her stretcher?

Then Colonel Merle had one of his great fits of rage—he roared and cursed and rushed along the corridor. Later, he, my father, and Monsieur Guyonnet left our compartment for long conferences with other members of the Armagnac group. At dusk, still in a state of extreme agitation, we reached Niort.

Like everyone around me, I felt sorry for the Kalitas. The FFIs were said to be vengeful against collaborators. Yet I was at last vindicated, and I felt pleasure. Clara's villainy finally had been demonstrated. Everyone was saying: "How could she do it?" and I felt like saying: "Hadn't you noticed, all those years? She is a witch."

However, I said nothing: my parents were very upset. A foreigner like ourselves, Clara had been a member of our clan. They had believed that Clara, like Paul, would fall in with the mood of trust that prevailed among the refugees.

The station in Niort, like the one in La Rochelle, had been heavily damaged by bombardments, yet it functioned even without the well-organized Germans to run it. Niort was a large railway center in those days. From my window seat, I looked out at the brightly lit station—air raids were no longer feared.

Natasha and André lived somewhere nearby. Perhaps the Sossinskys and my grandmother had disembarked on this platform the day before? What if we, too, could disembark here? What a joy it would be to see André and Natasha again! But unfortunately, as soon as we had come to a stop, a loudspeaker announced that no one, without exception, was to get off the train, which would be proceeding. Warm food would be served to the refugees.

Within minutes, a makeshift kitchen appeared on the platform—this time it curved to the right, and I could not see Clara's compartment. Through our lowered windows, Red Cross attendants passed tin mugs of hot soup. Armed FFI soldiers climbed aboard the train and checked papers. When they reached our compartment and were told that members of the Réseau Armagnac on Oléron had a report to make to the French authorities, they allowed my father, the colonel, Monsieur Guyonnet, and Monsieur Dupeux to go to their headquarters just outside the station.

Despite the confusion that followed the Kalitas' arrest, the four had evolved a plan of action. Colonel Merle and Monsieur Dupeux were to make a report on Armagnac activities on Oléron, especially on the Russians' readiness to risk their lives for the liberation of the island. My father and Monsieur Guyonnet were to go to the police station, to try to reach Surgère by telephone and establish Andrei Kalita's membership in Armagnac. Perhaps the Kalitas would then be released. After that, if he had time, my father would try to convince the authorities to let us leave the train at Niort since we had relatives there.

All four men returned within an hour. Monsieur Dupeux and Colonel Merle looked pleased: they had been received enthusiastically and were able to file a secret document about Armagnac on Oléron. My father said that there was no possibility of our staying in Niort. The region was so crowded with refugees that the French authorities, fearing famine and epidemic, had closed it off completely. On the other hand, he and Monsieur Guyonnet were hopeful about the Kalitas. The FFIs had been willing to acknowledge Kalita's Resistance credentials: in their presence, a French FFI captain had telephoned Surgère. The Kalitas would be freed at once and put on a train following ours.

"False denunciations usually come from people who are themselves guilty," the FFI captain had said. "Your Madame Rittoni must have things to hide. Let me look into the matter." My father and Monsieur Guyonnet had kept silent. The FFIs were said to be merciless to women who were suspected of having collaborated with the Germans. Horrifying stories on the subject had circulated on Oléron since the beginning of the Liberation. Fortunately, at that moment the FFI captain had been summoned elsewhere, and the matter was dropped.

We were leaving Niort, the train was accelerating, taking us south. Suddenly Colonel Merle leaned over my father and said something in a voice which was drowned by the wheels' clanging.

My father jumped up, yelling, "No!" He rushed to the window, lowering it with a bang, looking out into the fast-moving darkness. "No, no," he was shouting, turning back and looking at the colonel. I had never seen him so angry—he was shaking. He shouted, "How could you do it?"

And the colonel, smiling and looking once again like a Cheshire cat, kept repeating: "But you know that she is a public menace, Monsieur Andreyev!" In Niort, along with a statement about Armagnac, he and Monsieur Dupeux had filed a report about Clara's false denunciation against a member of the Resistance. Seconds before the train's departure, Clara and Paul had been arrested in a replay of the events in Surgère, unseen by us because of the curving platform.

The wheels were clanging, and I no longer felt vindicated. I had that feeling of nausea which I had felt that day in the fall of 1940, when I had discovered how much I loathed Clara. Now she had poisoned our first hours in freedom. The feeling stayed with me for days, intruding on the joy of our escape from the fortress Oléron.

In the little town of Saint-Sever in the foothills of the Pyrénées, where we had finally gotten off the train after a ride of more than one hundred hours, we received a letter from Natasha. It came in response to a telegram we had sent to her in Niort, telling her of our whereabouts. In this letter, my aunt told us that they were all well, that they had survived the spring bombardments of Niort by living out in the open fields for several weeks. The Sossinskys and my grandmother had arrived safely a few days before. Volodia had immediately joined the FFI in Niort, helping the French authorities handle the stray Russians brought into that region by the Germans, either as soldiers or as forced laborers. In her letter Natasha wrote:

> You will not believe this, but four days ago Clara and Paul made a brief appearance at our house. It went like this, a coincidence worthy of our high adventures during the Revolution. The evening after the Sossinskys and Mother arrived, Volodia was out at the FFI headquarters in town. He overheard a conversation between two FFI officers, talking about a blonde woman from the island of Oléron who had just been arrested. She was Italian—she had been the Germans' interpreter there and an avowed collaborator. Volodia knew at once that they were talking about Clara. He also knew what lies in store for women accused of collaboration with the Germans. He rushed to the local prison and had Clara and Paul released on the spot on his responsibility. Clara had not been molested—not yet. She and Paul came straight

to our house. They were scared and hungry and had lost all their luggage. Their belts and shoelaces had been taken. They were in a great hurry to leave—I gave them money for trainfare. They told us they were going to Paris. Why was Clara arrested? Who among the Oléronais was wicked enough to denounce her as a collaborator?"

Clara went out of our lives after this. I thought at the time that only Volodia's stubborn vocation as a knight-protector of widows and children could explain this coincidence, nothing short of miraculous for her. Perhaps Volodia's generosity exorcised her powers over us once and for all.

After the war, our family returned to Le Plessis near Paris and lived there happily for a long time. The Kalitas, freed by the FFIs in Surgère on that day in January 1945, joined us in the town of Saint-Sever. Then they returned to Paris and, like Clara, disappeared from our lives. I was to see Clara only once again. One evening in the fifties I was walking with my future husband, Henry Carlisle, in the Latin Quarter in Paris. I suddenly felt faint and reached for his arm. In the distance, Clara had crossed the Place Saint Germain, melting into the darkness.

In the early spring of 1976, I went back to Oléron with Sasha for the first time in many years. Oléron and Saint-Denis had greatly changed. But when we walked around Saint-Denis at night we recognized everything. The laurels still billow in black waves over the white stucco walls along Clara's lane, which curves ever so slightly as it reaches rue du Port. The jetty stands at the end of that street, eroded by the surf at its end, in that spot from which Clara used to dive into the sea like a siren, under the admiring eyes of the German officers. From the outside, the Maison Ardeber looks dark and mysterious, unaltered except that the yucca and the great chestnut are gone. A ridiculous grille has been installed atop the low stone wall on which the little boys used to sit. The "thinking wall" is still there, and one of the plum trees.

Our efforts to find people we had known on the island were not successful. The old people of Saint-Denis were gone. The young had grown old and had changed so much that we did not recognize them, nor they us. By one of those coincidences Saint-Denis had lavished on us in our childhood, Monsieur Guyonnet, who lived in retirement in Rochefort and with whom we were to visit on our way back from Oléron to Paris, died in his sleep on the very day my brother and I spent roaming around the island. Early that day, which was sunny and brisk, we found Mademoiselle Charles's shiny black marble gravestone in the cemetery, and I gave her my silent thanks for all the good things she had done for us in her own disorganized fashion. Nettles still grow in the ditch that surrounds the cemetery. There are fewer unused grassy spots within its walls.

We tried to find Julien, who works in the *étude de notaire* in Méray, now owned by a Maître Lambert. After a few months in Paris immediately after the war, he came back to live with his mother in Méray. Maître Lutin had died suddenly in 1946. From one day to another, Julien had given up what could have been a promising literary career in Paris. Madame Lutin wanting, perhaps unconsciously, to bring her son back to the island, had had some of his poems published on her own initiative by a provincial vanity press—to make him *une bonne surprise*. At that time, through the efforts of my grandmother, the distinguished publishing house of Gallimard had shown a readiness to launch Julien as a poet, but Madame Lutin's surprise put an end to that.

Sasha and I had looked for Julien all over the island throughout the day. As elusive as ever, still unmarried, he was out of his office whenever we dropped by. He was not at home when we called on him there, yet in both places everyone told us that he had been there only minutes before, and that he was to return at once. We waited a long time in his office in Maître Lambert's *étude*, where everything evoked his presence—the opened package of Gauloises, a disorderly pile of manuscripts, the multicolored folders marked in his handwriting, like those that used to surround Maître Lutin on Wednesdays when he held office hours in the Mairie. With unexpected intensity I was reminded with what desperation I had waited in vain for him at the Maison Ardeber—for days, for weeks, for years on end.

Julien did not return to his office that afternoon. After a while, Sasha and I decided to drive to the Lutins' house to pay our respects to Madame Lutin. Well into her eighties, Julien's mother was as sharp as ever, and as witty. She was no longer plump, but otherwise she had changed little. Her fine profile was still that of a sixteenth-century French dowager. She recognized Sasha at once but was unable to place me, thinking at first that I might be Sasha's wife. She had forgotten that there was a girl in our family. "Really? Did they have a girl?" she said. Otherwise she remembered our family vividly and warmly. She only made an exception for my grandmother, who with her customary excess of good feelings had tried to help Julien too enthusiastically with his literary affairs in Paris after the war. "Yes, she was very original. She did not try to understand our ways. She was, well—a Russian revolutionary," she said when she heard that my grandmother had died peacefully in Russia a few months after having returned there on an impulse in 1965.

Before leaving the island, as the sunlight was growing golden, my brother and I took a walk on the beach at Vert-Bois. The beach there is as beautiful as ever, unchanged since the 1940s, except for a line of litter mixed in with the seaweed at the tide's edge. There are big black balls of hardened tar scattered here and there among the snowy round rocks of the wild shore of Oléron. Otherwise it is as it used to be, as grandiose as ever. The waves still race each other with a great roaring as the tide comes in imperceptibly. There is a bracing smell of iodine in the air.

I asked Sasha whether he recalled our first day on the

island—the beach at Vert-Bois. He said he did, but only in the vaguest way. But he remembered people vividly, especially our Russian friends, Leva, Misha, and Ivan Petrovich. We had been reminded of them throughout the day in many spots once beloved by us—on Côte Sauvage, on Grande Plage, and along the chalky cliffs of La Morelière—where the Germans had built their fortifications. Parts of the cement bastions of the Atlantic wall have withstood thirty years of Oléron's weather. They look outsized and ghostly, staring blindly at the sea. Like our memories, they are fragmented and eroded. Someday they will be ground down to sand again. But the Russians are still remembered on Oléron: Rybov, who was detained in Eleanor's castle in Le Château, did not denounce his comrades, although it appears that he was roughed up, perhaps even tortured. Leva and two others who died during the liberation of Oléron are buried in the Saint-Pierre cemetery, where flowers are placed on their graves on All Saints' Day.

Shortly before the German surrender, in the spring of 1945, the island was freed by a detachment of the Resistance network Armagnac. It included some of the men who had worked in the underground against the Germans in our region. This military campaign gave both the French Free Forces and our Russians from Russia that ultimate satisfaction, an open combat with the Germans. Volodia was there with Armagnac. He arrived in La Perroche moments after Leva, whom my grandmother had once seen as a hero, was shot by the Germans. He was caught sabotaging one of their mortars. For our Russians, this moment of glory was followed by disaster. Their motherland did not welcome them when they returned. Nearly all of them were arrested by Stalin's police on charges of having plotted against his life while abroad, with my father, Vadim

Andreyev, as their main accomplice and organizer. But that is another story that too shall not be forgotten—stories like that stay alive as long as there is a Russia.

After Stalin's death, Volodia went to live in Moscow. He was able to trace several of the Russians from Oléron, notably Misha Dudin and Ivan Petrovich. As chivalrous as ever and as energetic, he helped them gain rehabilitation from the imaginary accusations that had sent them to labor camps. Once again, he was able to make a bridge between their Russia and our own, that of long ago on the island of Oléron. I, however, was never to see any of our friends again. Nor is it likely that I ever will, but then we all have come home, each in our way. Or have we? Russians are the wanderers of our time. We all dream of reaching that luminous island where curly-headed vineyards run out to sea.

It took me a long time to decipher the secret meaning of our years on Oléron. Like the treasure hidden in Mademoiselle Charles's grove, it kept eluding me.

As a young woman I left France for the United States. I lived among Americans, some of whom were writers. They resembled the Russians of my early years—they too were searching for their lost country, their childhood. In New York I studied painting. I also went to Moscow as a literary journalist. I tried to share with my American friends what I knew of Russia.

Over the years, in conversations, I told my friends about our island, about the endless sea-lulled days waiting for the war to end; about the intrusions, the Germans' and Clara's, whose malevolent hold over my feelings had at last been exorcised by my uncle. Yet in my mind the memories of Oléron remained ambiguous, like the beach at Vert-Bois, which was both a gift of freedom and a threat, as the waves there move imperceptibly toward one.

Then one day on a beach in California, looking out at the sea, I was thinking again of Vert-Bois, and I understood: Oléron was more than an episode in an émigré's life, more than a long interlude of waiting for the war to end. It was more than sunny memories turned into a necklace of dead bees. Oléron was for me a special island in time, life-strengthening like my father's garden, ever renewed like the tides on Grande Plage. Oléron meant promises and many hard choices, which my parents helped me learn how to make. Both promises and choices still stretch out before me like Clara's lane in the velvety darkness, an unknown future to which I must give shape.